Communicating Projects

This book is dedicated to my best friend Jo Hodgkinson (1962–2012)

Communicating Projects

An End-to-End Guide
to Planning, Implementing
and Evaluating Effective
Communication

ANN PILKINGTON

GOWER

Published by
Gower Publishing Limited
Wey Court East
Union Road
Farnham
Surrey, GU9 7PT
England

Ashgate Publishing Company
110 Cherry Street
Suite 3-1
Burlington, VT 05401-3818
USA

www.gowerpublishing.com

British Library Cataloguing in Publication Data
A catalogue record for this book is available from the British Library.

Library of Congress Cataloging-in-Publication Data
Pilkington, Ann.
  Communicating projects : an end-to-end guide to planning, implementing and evaluating effective communication / by Ann Pilkington.
    pages cm
  Includes bibliographical references and index.
  ISBN 978-1-4094-5319-2 (hardback) -- ISBN 978-1-4094-5320-8 (ebook) --
ISBN 978-1-4724-0832-7 (epub) 1. Project management. 2. Communication in management.
I. Title.
  HD69.P75P536 2013
  658.4'5--dc23

                                                                               2013023799

ISBN 978-1-4094-5319-2 (hardback)
ISBN 978-1-4094-5320-8 (PDF – ebook)
ISBN 978-1-4724-0832-7 (PDF – epub)

Printed in the United Kingdom by Henry Ling Limited,
at the Dorset Press, Dorchester, DT1 1HD

Contents

List of Figures

List of Tables

Foreword

I am delighted and honoured to be able to write this introduction to Ann's excellent book. There is a need for it, for project managers everywhere communications are an important but often neglected competency. To have understandable guidance from a true expert is of real value.

Some examples of why we need to improve project communications:

1.   In the past few weeks I have attended conferences and heard a variety of speakers talking about the problems that Chief Executive Officers regard as most pressing. Top of the list comes 'Management of Change' – and when we explore why is this so difficult, the issue is one of keeping people informed and persuading them to co-operate.

2.   Every staff survey that is produced in companies around the world has a major theme in the results, 'Nobody keeps us informed, we are not consulted'.

3.   At one time, I worked in a company that, twice a year, held a briefing for all staff on what was happening in the Company, the financial state of the business, future work, etc. – it was a veritable state of the nation address and took half a day. It was a big meeting and so we had to cross town to a large venue and the journey was done in buses. I knew how much work had gone into the presentations, the time that had been spent making sure that the wording was correct and yet on the return to the site as I listened to the conversations around me, the people could have all been to different meetings. Human beings have a wonderful capacity to hear what they want to hear and vice versa.

These examples have a common theme, the difficulty of effective communication. The problem is acute in projects for a variety of reasons. Very few projects have enough resources to have a communications specialist and the job is often left to be done if, and when, someone remembers.

One of the techniques that I use to collect lessons from projects is to hold a project history workshop. It is remarkable how so many of the same project team have a different view of what happened and why.

In recent years it has been recognised that effective project management depends heavily on people, team members, stakeholders. Effective communications are required to use these resources to the best advantage.

So, read this book, learn from it and never again be tempted to say *"But I told you"*. We all have to stop ourselves from operating in 'Transmit Mode'.

Thank you Ann for sharing your wisdom with us.

Mary McKinlay FAPM
Trustee and Board Member APM
Adjunct Professor, SKEMA France

Preface

It is acknowledged widely that good communication is important to project success but what does good project communication look like? This book sets out to answer this question with guidance that will be useful for the project manager and the project communicator.

Large-scale projects will probably have the luxury of an experienced communication team and the ability to draw in additional resources as and when needed. On smaller projects however, communication can be the remit of a very small team or maybe even just one person, sometimes given the role without having had any previous communication experience.

This presents a risk to project success, particularly when communication is viewed as a one-way activity that is more about 'sending out stuff' than true two-way engagement with stakeholders.

Successful communication results from strategic planning and relies on knowledge of appropriate theory. Anyone who has worked in a project environment will, at some time, have experienced frustration because stakeholders claim not to know what is happening, what they need to do or are simply antagonistic. Of course it will never be possible to please all of the stakeholders all of the time, but an understanding of how people process communication will help.

The book is designed to be of value to those given a project communication task but without previous communication experience. It also acts as a guide for project managers in terms of knowing what to expect from the communication work that they commission.

For the more experienced communicator, the book can be useful in terms of setting the communication role in the context of a project with its particular requirements in terms of documentation, reporting and supporting the delivery of milestones. For the communicator working at programme level, the same principles of good communication apply and where appropriate, reference is made to the different requirements of programme or portfolio communication.

The book provides an end-to-end guide from the establishment of the communication function through to the evaluation of communication activity. It is also structured in such a way to enable the communicator to find guidance on one particular aspect of communication.

The book is written from the perspective of a project that is happening within a wider organisation, but where this isn't the case, much of the guidance can still be followed in order to deliver successful communication.

Because an understanding of theory is so important for any successful communication there are a number of Vignettes throughout where an aspect of theory is discussed in more depth. These sections can only provide an overview of each concept, but the references included can guide the reader to further reading.

On a more practical level, the book provides a number of template plans plus hints and tips as part of a Project Communicator's Toolkit.

Throughout the book communication concepts are mapped on to the project lifecycle. The model used is that from the *Association of Project Managers' Body of Knowledge 6th Edition*. However most communication activity will begin towards the end of the definition stage, continuing through development and into handover. The development phase can sometimes – according to the project – be broken down further, often into design, build and test, and this is also illustrated in some of the models given.

Chapter 1: This chapter discusses the different options for setting up a communication function. It makes the case for communication to be seen as a strategic function, not just tactical and discusses the differences between the two forms of communication together with the skills and competencies required.

For the communicator, one of the biggest challenges can often be gaining an understanding of the project that is detailed enough to enable a suitable communication strategy to be designed. This chapter contains advice on the approach to take and the questions to ask. It goes on to provide guidance on some of the requirements of working in a project environment, such as documentation.

Chapter 2: With the foundations of the communication function in place, this chapter takes the reader through the strategic planning process. The chapter emphasises the importance of planning and thinking strategically before beginning to develop content and communicating. Without this phase communication activity will be unfocussed and unlikely to help the project hit its milestones and realise its benefits. Creating content and communication materials is often thought to be the creative phase, but in fact it is at this strategic stage when the communicator carries out analysis and uses this to inform the strategic approach that real creativity is applied.

Some elements of that process are worthy of deeper discussion and these aspects are discussed in the following chapters.

Chapter 3: In this chapter, the case is made for communication to either take the lead in managing stakeholder engagement or at the very least be at the heart of the process. A structured process to working with stakeholders is outlined.

Chapter 4: Having undertaken all the necessary analysis and done the strategic thinking, it is time to start developing the content. Both written and verbal communication are discussed with hints and tips provided for both.

Chapter 5: Selecting the right channel, or method of communication, matters. The channel becomes part of the message so must be appropriate to the content. For example, where email may be suitable for short non-controversial messages, nobody wants to hear news of changes to their job in this way. It is also essential to match the channel to the communication strategy or approach that has been selected. A range of different channels is given and guidance on whether they are one-way or two-way is provided.

Chapter 6: Planning is one of those activities that often gets put to one side on the basis that there isn't time to do it but in a project environment this isn't acceptable nor is it desirable. Communication activity must be planned in order to fall in line with project milestones and feed into wider project planning. The chapter talks through a range of different plans, which can look rather daunting, but planning doesn't have to be onerous. Lengthy, complex plans are more likely to become out of date and fail to be useful. Keep them short and simple and they are more likely to aid delivery.

Chapter 7: Although this chapter on research and evaluation comes at the end, research has a role to play throughout the life of the project. It is used to inform the communication strategy right at the start, in conducting evaluation as the activity is being delivered (to ensure it is working) and at the end when the results can be fed into lessons learned.

*****

The goal of this book is not only to provide communicators with practical help and guidance but to help to raise the profile of communication within the project setting as a strategic function. When communication sits at the project board table, is planned strategically and evaluated properly it is more likely to contribute to project success and be a far more rewarding role for the communicator.

Acknowledgements

Thanks must go to Lou Horton for sharing her ideas (particularly on stakeholder models), support and honest feedback. Also to my husband Kevin Ruck for his support and tolerance throughout the writing process. I am grateful to the team at Pillory Barn Creative for turning my scrawled models into something legible.

Setting Out

Project communication, where to start? For the project manager, there is no doubt that communication matters, but what does good project communication look like? Where should it sit within the project structure? What type of skills and competencies are needed? How does it differ from other communication disciplines, for example internal communication and public relations (PR)?

For the communicator, it can be daunting to arrive on a project at any stage of its lifecycle. There is a requirement to get up to speed quickly with what the project is delivering, understand the structure as well as the politics and often pressure is applied to start delivering communication activity immediately. However, the temptation to jump straight in to communicating should be resisted.

Good project communication is built on clarity, not just clarity of message, but clarity of role. Time spent in the early stages of a project agreeing the role of communication and being clear about both what it is and isn't there to do is time well spent. The ideal scenario is for the project communicator to be part of the project from the outset, but where this isn't the case and communication is brought in a little further through the lifecycle, time should still be taken to ensure that there is a common understanding of the role and that it is structured in the most appropriate way.

This chapter set outs to help the project manager or the communicator tasked with establishing or reviewing the function by first discussing what good communication looks like before moving on to cover:

- different communication disciplines;

- the difference between strategic and technical communication;

- how to scope the communication requirement;

- the structure of the communication function;

- communication responsibilities across the project;

- project documentation;

- gaining an understanding of the project;

- key relationships for communicators.

These are the foundations of a good project communication function and need to be in place before the strategy is created and communication activity is undertaken.

What Does Good Project Communication Look Like?

To answer this question, it is necessary to first think about what communication actually is. Despite the fact that projects exist in a world of sophisticated media and advertising, there is still a tendency for communication to be thought of as a simply linear process, that is, somebody is told something, they interpret it in the way that was intended by the sender and that is all that is needed. Where this 'send out stuff' approach still prevails on projects it is no wonder that stakeholders are cynical or disengaged and projects don't realise their benefits.

Of course in reality the communication process is a lot richer than that. The way that someone interprets a message is influenced by many things: culture, the perception of the sender, the way the message is sent, the recipient's mood on the day or the environment. In the context of a project, stakeholders' perceptions of the project and what it is setting out to achieve can influence the way that messages are interpreted. Once this is understood, it becomes clear why so often communication doesn't work in the way that was intended and why communication is anything but a soft skill.

So, effective communication relies on an understanding of this complexity and on being able to design communication tactics that take account of the environment. This turns it into a strategic function – not simply tactical. The communicator has a range of tools in his or her tool box, but selecting the right one at the right time is only achieved based on an understanding of the richness and complexity of the communication process. There is more on the richness of communication in the Vignette on communication theory.

In order to be effective at a strategic level, the project communicator needs to have gravitas and confidence in his or her capabilities. Projects are often led by strong characters – just the trait needed when there is a difficult job to be done – but that doesn't always bring with it an understanding of communication and it can feel difficult to challenge – especially for the lone practitioner. However, sometimes an effective, well articulated challenge will be needed in order to get the right outcome for the project.

In the same way that a project manager relies on any specialist for advice (Human Resources (HR), finance and so on), he or she needs to be able to call on their communication lead to provide strategic counsel. The communication function is there to help ensure that the project hits its milestones and delivers its benefits. It does this by:

- scoping and understanding the communication requirement;

- developing and maintaining a fit-for-purpose communication strategy and plan;

- taking an audience/stakeholder-centred approach;

- ensuring there is a clear vision and narrative;

- coaching and advising projects leaders on personal communication style and messaging;

- providing accurate and timely information;

- encouraging and facilitating feedback to help achieve mutual understanding between the project and its stakeholders;

- producing communication products that are accurate, on-brand and meet a communication need;

- evaluating the effectiveness of communication;

- building relationships with other communicators;

- monitoring the environment to 'gauge the mood' of stakeholders.

In defining the scope of communication it is also important to consider what it isn't there to do. The communication function is not there to:

- be a substitute for good governance;

- massage the ego of the project manager or sponsors (although a bit of that might be in order from time to time);

- absolve line managers of their responsibility to communicate with their teams;

- manage project documentation;

- make a bad decision look like a good one;

- fix things that aren't communication problems.

In summary, the best project communication draws on the theory of communication, operates at strategic level, provides advice when needed and never simply 'sends out stuff'.

The Different Communication Disciplines

Project communication doesn't fit neatly into any of the traditional communication disciplines, instead it draws from all of them and that's what makes it rewarding, challenging and distinct. However, it can also make project communication hard to define, with this leading to confusion within the project about what it is there to do.

The main communication disciplines are defined in Table 1.1. Understanding the different disciplines is helpful for three main reasons:

- Using the right terminology helps ensure there is a shared understanding of what the communication function is there to do. For example, most people are familiar with the term marketing

– although often it is used to mean promotional marketing communication. The danger for the project communicator who is asked to 'market' the project is that it has a high association with persuasion, that is, the 'selling' of products, services or ideas. Of course, every project wants people to buy in to its objectives and be willing to adapt their behaviour (for example in the workplace by adopting a new business process) but it is simplistic to think that this can be achieved through promotional messaging alone.

- Being clear about the different communication disciplines is helpful in understanding how communication activity is structured in the wider organisation of which the project is a part.

- Depending on the size and objectives of the project, specialist communication activity may need to be commissioned.

Table 1.1   Communication disciplines defined

Advertising	Traditionally advertising is paid for messaging and is one-way, although opportunities presented through social media mean that advertising practitioners are increasingly involved in more innovative ways to reach their audiences.
Employee engagement	Employee engagement is a fairly new discipline and sometimes sits within HR rather than within a communication team. However, good communication is essential to employee engagement. There is still no one agreed definition but in a study commissioned by the UK Government in 2009 – Engaging for Success – MacLeod and Clarke concluded that the best way to look at it was as a workplace approach designed to ensure that employees are committed to their organisation's goals and values, motivated to contribute to organisational success, and are able at the same time to enhance their own sense of well-being.
Internal (employee) communication	Internal communication is the subset of PR that looks after employees. Although traditionally often a one-way function concerned only with telling employees things, it is increasingly concerned with facilitating a dialogue with employees and contributing to employee engagement.
Marketing	The Chartered Institute of Marketing explains marketing as: 'The management process responsible for identifying, anticipating and satisfying customer requirements profitably.' The term marketing is often used incorrectly to mean sales or promotion of a product. In fact these are different disciplines although are part of the marketing mix.
Marketing communication	Marketing communication – sometimes referred to as 'marcomms' is the discipline associated with the 'promotion' element of the marketing mix also known as the 4Ps: product, price, place, promotion. There is no recognised definition and its roles are only becoming harder to define as social media blurs the boundaries between the communication disciplines. Practitioners of marketing communication may be involved in advertising, branding, media relations, social media campaigns and the production of collateral such as brochures.

Table 1.1   Continued

Media relations	The subset of PR that looks after relationships with the media. In large organisations, there may be a press office function which is largely reactive, handling enquiries from journalists. However media relations is also proactive with practitioners working to place stories about their organisations in the media and build relationships with journalists, bloggers and so on.
Public Relations (PR). Can also be called Corporate Communication	The UK Chartered Institute of Public Relations defines it as: 'The discipline which looks after reputation, with the aim of earning understanding and support and influencing opinion and behaviour. It is the planned and sustained effort to establish and maintain goodwill and mutual understanding between an organisation and its publics.' PR practice can encompass internal communication, public affairs, financial PR, corporate social responsibility (CSR) and media relations. PR is sometimes presented as being about a two-way dialogue with stakeholders (the term 'publics' is used in this definition) but in reality, many PR practitioners practice one-way communication and the work is often largely media based.

Project Communication: Strategic and Technical

The communication practitioner role can be thought about at two levels: strategic and technical (see Figure 1.1). Each is dependent on the other. Good technical communication (for example, newsletter production) is only effective when it delivers a strategy and a strategy is only effective when it is delivered by well thought through technical communication. No project leader is going to take communication seriously at a strategic level if the team can't produce an accurate distribution list or a web page without typographical errors. The project needs both skills sets, either in a team or in an individual. Table 1.2 outlines the distinction between the strategic and the technical.

Table 1.2   Communication skills and competencies

Skills and competencies	
Communicator as strategic adviser	**Communicator as technician**
• Is comfortable working at board level; • provides strategic counsel; • has well developed stakeholder management and influencing skills; • understands how to use research to inform strategy; • draws on latest theory and thinking to inform practice; • speaks the language of business; • builds effective relationships.	• Has good written communication skills; • is experienced at managing a range of channels and tactics; • understands the management of design and print projects; • works accurately with attention to detail; • understands project methodology.

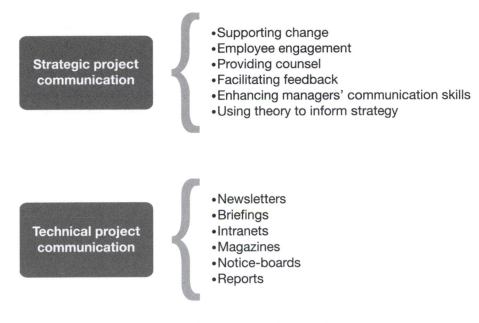

Figure 1.1   Project communication is both strategic and technical

STRATEGIC PROJECT COMMUNICATION

The project communicator acting at a strategic level:

- Is comfortable working at board level. The communication function should ideally be represented at the senior table and be involved in the strategic discussions around the project. It is important to hear first-hand what senior sponsors are thinking and gain an awareness of the politics of the programme. Advising the right communication approach is difficult if there isn't awareness and understanding of what may be going on in the background. Project boards should look to their communication lead to provide counsel as decisions are being made rather than simply expecting them to just tell everyone once something is decided. Good decisions factor in the communication implications. However, to do this effectively, communicators must be comfortable operating at this level and have the respect of the senior team. This means that the project communicator must have sufficient grading or standing within the project and the wider organisation of which the project is a part.

- Provides strategic counsel. This is what makes the real difference to project communication – a practitioner who can get to grips quickly with the issues, knows the right questions to ask and offers advice accordingly. The project communicator needs to earn the trust and respect of the senior project team in order to fulfil this role effectively, but there is also an onus on the project leadership to seek out advice on the communication aspects of decisions as they are being made. This sometimes means that there needs to be a step change in the way that communication is viewed by project managers, moving away from it being about sending out messages to being a much more strategic function.

- Has well developed stakeholder management and influencing skills. It is all very well for the communicator to know the right answer, but ensuring that his or her voice is heard and the advice followed can be more of a challenge. A seat at the top table helps, bringing as it does insights and understanding of stakeholders' perspectives. The communicator has to earn the trust of the senior team but this only comes about over time. Using research-based evidence to show why something did or didn't work is helpful. Knowing the right time to challenge is important. While trust is being built, it may be advisable to save challenge for the more important issues but always ensure there is evidence from theory, best practice or research to support the point being made.

- Understands how to use research to inform strategy. The best communication strategies are grounded in research. This doesn't have to be expensive or onerous. Understanding the right research approach and how to interpret the results leads to more effective outcomes and saves time, effort and therefore money. Less can be more in communication. There is more about research for communication in Chapter 7.

- Draws on latest theory and thinking to inform practice. Gone are the days when a 'seat-of-the-pants' approach to communication was acceptable. Like research, an understanding of theory can prevent effort being wasted on ineffective or potentially damaging communication. The effective communicator needs an understanding that spans areas such as communication theory, psychology and employee engagement.

- Speaks the language of the business. Sitting at the top table is all very well, but once there, the communicator needs to be able to talk the language of business in order to be taken seriously. That means understanding the corporate strategy, the balance sheet, the business case for the project and the environment in which the project and the organisation of which it is a part operates. Without this, communicators will struggle to have influence and to get communication taken seriously as a strategic function.

- Builds effective relationships. The communication role will span all areas of a project and also span the boundry between the project and the environment around it. Relationships need to built at all levels, not just upwards, and also with those beyond the project. There is more on relationship building later in this chapter.

TECHNICAL PROJECT COMMUNICATION

The technical project communicator:

- Has good written communication skills. For many years, being able to write well was the measure by which communicators were judged; and it remains important. Good writing skills mean the ability to construct a story, think about the audience and write clearly and simply without jargon.

- Is experienced at managing a range of channels and tactics. Project communication can involve a wide variety of different tactics and channels with different approaches being used at different project stages. This might include organising focus groups, workshops or events, setting up web pages, producing e-bulletins or newsletters and managing social media channels.

- Understands the management of design and print projects: most project communication will call for some design work and production of collateral. Design is a specialist skill and should be done by specialists. Amateur design always looks just that – amateur. The communicator's role is to commission and brief a designer then manage the work through to completion on time, on budget and on brand.

- Works accurately with attention to detail. It is worth emphasising what should be an obvious point because there is no quicker way to undermine the credibility of the communication function than with inaccurate distribution lists and misspelling of names.

- Understands project methodology. This can of course be learned, but the key is to work in a planned way, appreciating the dependencies that communication has on other parts of the project and the dependencies that there are on communication. Again, it is an important part of the communication function gaining credibility within the project. Delivering project documentation on time and to the required standard again sounds obvious, but it matters for the success of the project and the reputation of the communication function.

Scoping the Communication Need

Being clear from the start about the communication need ensures that the right communication resource is brought in at the right time. The need for communication is not necessarily driven by the scale or cost of a project; for example a low-cost project may be delivering a substantial or controversial change that will need considerable communication resource.

Key questions to ask are:

- What is the impact of the change on each stakeholder group? Defining the impact is generally the responsibility of the business change function, but at the start of a project, this team may not be in place or the work may not have been done. If this is the case, it makes sense to wait until it has been completed before making a final decision on the type and amount of communication resources needed.

- Is the project likely to be of interest outside the organisation of which it is a part? Will this mean potential media and political interest?

- How controversial is the project likely to be? For example, are jobs being removed or changed? Is there likely to be an impact on the environment?

- Are stakeholders generally favourable or are there pressure groups with views about the project?

- How complex will it be to deliver?

- What are the implications of it going wrong?

- Is there any political sensitivity?

- What is the impact of the change – will people be asked to make a significant change in behaviour?

- How many people are affected?

- Is the organisation accustomed to handling change?

Think about how the requirement will vary at different times through the lifecycle. For example, at the outset, the need may be for a high level of stakeholder engagement, with this reducing as the project moves towards roll out. Getting ready for roll out may call for greater input and more technical skills, for example in the production of communication materials (brochures, intranets, events and so on).

Where Does Communication Sit? How is it Structured?

There are some choices to make in terms of where communication resources come from:

- draw on central, corporate resource from the organisation of which the project is a part;

- dedicated resource, located within the project structure, a role with a finite life.

Of course there are factors that may dictate the choice made, for example:

- budget available;

- duration of project;

- recruitment polices of the organisation of which the project is a part;

- the scale of the communication need (the emphasis here is purposefully on the *communication* need; a project that is costing a lot does not necessarily equal large-scale communication requirements).

There is no right or wrong answer. Table 1.3 sets out some of the key considerations.

Table 1.3   Communication function structure: corporate resource versus project resource

Corporate resource versus project resource		
	Pros	**Cons**
Central corporate resource	• Reduced line management responsibility (although matrix management may apply); • increased opportunities for synergies and alignment with corporate messages and activity; • likely to have access to a wide range of skills and experience within the corporate communication team; • flexibility of resource; • potentially cheaper.	• Without strong service level agreements, potential lack of control; • risk that work will not be prioritised; • lack of understanding of the particular demands of project work; • time needed to brief on requirements.
Dedicated resource, located within the project structure	• Higher level of understanding of project; • more responsive; • no conflicting priorities; • appreciation of project environment and demands.	• Can be harder to join up messages with central activity; • line management demands; • ability to recruit for a finite term.

DEDICATED RESOURCE IN THE PROJECT STRUCTURE

If the decision is made to bring communication within the project, the next thing to think about is where it should sit within the structure. There are a few choices, including:

- as part of the project office;

- reporting directly to the project manager;

- as part of business change.

This chapter has set out how communication should be strategic as well as tactical and this is more likely to be achieved if it reports directly to the project manager. A project that sees communication as simply a function of the project office and there to send out messages risks missing the added value that the communication function can bring. If communication sits as part of another function it is reliant on others with a seat on the project board to identify communication needs and unless that person is an experienced communicator, important communication requirements could be missed.

One of the common challenges for communicators is colleagues within the project thinking that because something is significant to them, it will be to others. This isn't necessarily so and, conversely, it can be the case that there are decisions or developments which are seemingly small to the project, but could have a significant impact on stakeholders. It should be for communicators to decide what matters most, but to do that, they need access to the thinking and the decision making.

Locating communication within business change can work well. Successful business change relies on good communication with stakeholders and the close working that results from the two functions being together can help to bring this about.

There is a further model and that is one where the role shifts during the project lifecycle, starting out as a central, programme function and moving to become part of business change as the project moves towards implementation.

WHERE COMMUNICATION SITS: PROGRAMME PERSPECTIVE

Programmes are made up of a number projects that are all working together to deliver a particular outcome. The project and programme communication roles are very similar – the difference is often simply a question of scale. At the programme level, there will be a role to ensure that communication across its constituent projects is aligned. In the same way, communication at project level will be ensuring that this happens across all the constituent work streams.

Programme communication ensures this alignment by having oversight of project-level strategies and plans. The programme-level strategy comes first, with those at project level supporting the aims and objectives that it contains.

It may be the case that the communication needs of the constituent projects can be served from a central programme resource, this can be the most efficient model as the needs of an individual project will vary over the life of the programme and a full-time or permanent resource may not always be required. Alternatively, communicators can be positioned within the projects. The key with this latter model is for the central programme communication function to have the authority to provide direction to project communication. A consistency of message and approach is needed across a programme and the structure chosen must facilitate and support this.

The advantages of a central programme model where a team provides communication services for the programme and across the projects include:

- messages can be joined up across the programme's constituent projects more easily;

- resources can be focussed where the need is greatest at a particular time, making it more cost effective;

- it creates a supportive environment in which communicators work as part of a team rather than as individuals or in a number of very small, disparate teams;

- added value to the programme as potential conflicts and synergies across projects are spotted more easily (these may not always be communication related, but as communication in this model is uniquely placed in spanning all projects, it may notice things that would otherwise be missed).

Disadvantages include:

- project managers feeling that they have a lack of control over communication;

- inability to serve the needs of all projects when demand is high;

- potential for there to be a weaker understanding of an individual project.

Of course, in making any model work, much depends on personalities and individuals' experience and understanding of communications. With mutual respect and understanding either model can work well.

Communication: Who is Responsible for What?

Successful project communication relies on others within the project and those sponsoring it to play a role. Having agreed how communication will be structured, it can then be useful to set out what is expected of others in the project team. In all cases, there will probably be a role for the communication function to provide support. For example, while project sponsors will need to take some responsibility for stakeholder relations, it can be for the communication function to support them with work on the prioritisation of stakeholders, development of messages and materials to help them deliver those messages to the stakeholders with whom they have a relationship.

Mapping everyone's roles and responsibilities in relation to communication can be really valuable in ensuring that:

- everyone knows what is expected of them;

- gaps can be spotted;

- duplication of effort is avoided;

- stakeholders are less likely to be confused by multiple approaches from the project.

Every project will be different, but Table 1.4 acts as an example of how others on the project can support effective communication.

Table 1.4   **Communication responsibilities**

Role	Communication responsibility	Support from communication function
Sponsors	• Stakeholder relations (owns particular relationships); • uses opportunities to raise awareness and understanding of the project with their peers; • uses relationships to achieve specific outcomes for the project (for example business case approval).	• Stakeholder identification, allocation of ownership; • project key messages (relevant to the stakeholder); • tools and templates to help with tracking and monitoring of relationships.
Project manager	• Stakeholder relations (owns particular relationships); • leadership communication with the project team.	• Stakeholder identification, allocation of ownership; • project key messages (relevant to stakeholders and team); • tools and templates to help with tracking and monitoring of relationships; • plan for project team communication.
Project management office	• Project communication relating to project processes, documentation etc.; • in some circumstances can take on responsibility for communication within the project team.	• Collaborate on accurate distribution lists for the project; • provide guidance on branding of project documentation; • ensure messages are consistent and clear.
Work stream leads	• Stakeholder relations (as identified and agreed centrally with the project).	• Project key messages (relevant to stakeholder); • tailoring of messages as required.

Project Documentation

Having scoped the communication requirement and come to a decision about structure, the next stage is to capture everything in proper project documentation.

Some communicators may arrive on the project at this stage and it is likely that having got to understand the project (more on this later) they will be tasked with creating all the necessary documentation that sets out how communication will work. For someone experienced in communication, but not experienced in project work, this is likely to be something new – particularly if previous communication roles have been largely reactive. The discipline of creating project documentation is valuable and would be of benefit in any communication role.

The documentation that will be required for the communication function will depend on whether the project stands alone or is part of a programme. Within a programme, communication may be a project in its own right, be part of another project (for example business change) or it may not be set up as a project at all but report directly to the programme manager.

The documentation that the project communicator is likely to have to produce includes:

- the project initiation document or 'PID' (if communication is to be a project within a programme);

- the communication project plan (if, as above, within a programme) or inputs into a plan;

- risk and issues log;

- product description for the communication strategy and plan;

- and of course the communication strategy and plan itself.

Table 1.5   Summary of communication project documentation

Document	Purpose and content
Project initiation document	This sets out how the project will be run. The PMO should provide a template. It will include things like resources needed to deliver the strategy, scope, responsibilities, what the communication project is setting out to achieve. Outside of the project environment, much of what is contained here would go into a communication strategy (for example budget and resources required).
Project plan	The project plan is distinct from the communication plan. It sets out how the strategy and plan will be developed and delivered. For example, when sign-off of the strategy will be achieved, when it will be reviewed and updated, how and when the communication plan will be evaluated, production schedule for key communication materials.
Risk and issues register or log (this depends whether it is a standalone project, if not risks will be included in the owning-project risk register)	Guidance will be available from the project office on the format for capturing risks and issues – projects often have their own ranking and coding systems which should be followed. As a rule, the log is likely to include: who raised the risk, the severity of the risk, risk owner, mitigating action, status and updates.

The project documentation (PID and project plan) sets out how the communication strategy and plan will be developed and delivered and the communication strategy and plan set out how the communication itself will be delivered. There is more on developing the communication strategy in Chapter 2 and on developing plans in Chapter 6.

There may be some overlaps between the PID and the communication strategy, for example, objectives and scope, but essentially the PID is much more about how the communication function will operate than the communication activity itself.

RISKS AND ISSUES

It is helpful to start by explaining the terms 'risk' and 'issues'. Essentially, a risk is something that may happen and, if it does, have a negative impact on the project. An issue is something that is already happening. If a risk isn't spotted and addressed it can turn into an issue which is why the risk log or register is such an important project document.

The project risk and issues register can also be a really valuable way of getting the voice of communication heard. The clever communicator gets this tool to work for them. Once something is captured on the risk log then it is hard to ignore it. For example, there can sometimes be reluctance for project colleagues to share progress – particularly when things aren't going to well – or to simply give the communication function a low priority. If this is happening, consider raising it as a risk. After all, stakeholders will lose confidence if they aren't kept up to date and problems aren't acknowledged so this is a valid communication risk. Raise risks wisely and selectively though, the risk log is no substitute for building trusted relationships with colleagues.

The communication function is often a risk owner or communication is given as mitigation of risk. But do check that the risk or issue is within the gift of communication to resolve. This isn't about absolving communication of responsibility; it is about ensuring that the true risk or issue has been captured. For example, concerns among stakeholders that the project won't deliver may indeed be down to the need for greater communication, but it could be because there isn't a workable project plan in place. If the latter is the case it is a workable project plan that is needed, not just more communication.

How to Understand the Project

The first step to good project communication is to understand the project itself. It sounds simple and obvious, but can be challenging. Project communicators come up against some common barriers:

- project jargon, highly technical language or business speak;

- team members focussed on their own area of work and deadlines so not seeing the bigger picture;

- communication isn't given the status on the project that it deserves;

- project politics and egos;

- project leaders not wanting to admit to problems or delays;

- lack of a clear vision for the project.

So how can communicators overcome the barriers and get to the heart of what a project is setting out to achieve?

DO SOME READING: REVIEW THE PROJECT DOCUMENTS

All projects will have documentation that can help the communicator. It pays to spend time reviewing them. Depending on the size of the project and the project methodology being used, these may vary in name and nature, but here are some key ones to look out for. Key documents to review include:

- The business case: this should set out the rationale for the project and the benefits to be gained.

- The vision and blueprint: used in change projects, this will tell you what the project wants to achieve and what the organisation will be like when the project completes.

- Project initiation document (PID): this should set out things like the objectives for the project, the scope, assumptions, deliverables, resources and risks.

- The risks and issues register: communication should be contributing to this either in terms of raising risks or providing mitigation of risks. Reviewing the register is a quick way to understand any problems that the project may face.

- Project plans and roadmaps: these are useful in that they set out what will be achieved by when and the communication plan should of course be aligned with them.

- Lessons learned: has a similar project been done before? If so, review the lessons learned document.

ASK THE RIGHT PEOPLE

As the new communicator on a project, set up some short interviews with key project people. Start with the project manager and maybe ask their advice about whom else to talk to. Get their support for this so that others can see that it is a priority; perhaps he or she could mention it to people during a checkpoint meeting and ask them to make time available.

It is important to go into any such interview well prepared. Refer back to the project documentation and identify any gaps and points where more detail is needed to inform communication. People may try to save time and avoid answering questions by simply referring back to their documentation, so it is important to make it clear that this has been read, but that there is additional information or more explanation needed.

In addition to the project manager, good people to interview include:

- work stream leads (or project leads if it is a programme);

- benefits manager;

- head of the PMO;

- business change lead;

- senior sponsor (sometimes referred to as the SRO: senior responsible officer/owner).

Project colleagues will very often be specialists in their field and very focussed on what they have been asked to deliver – they don't always see the bigger picture, so communicators need to ask the right questions to get the information that they need. Simply asking somebody what they are doing may result in a complicated description of some technical process, leaving the communicator more confused than ever!

So, never just ask, 'What are you doing?' Some possible questions might be:

- Who will be affected by what you are doing – within the project and outside it? The external perspective is important – it is essential to know, for example, if there is an impact on peoples' jobs.

- On who or what are you dependent to deliver your work?

- Who is dependent on you?

- What does success look like?

- Ask how they would explain to their mum, a son or daughter what the project is doing – this can help to remove some of the jargon.

As part of this exercise, check that there is a common understanding of the vision. If there isn't, flag this to the project manager and work with him or her on a strategy to address it.

BE AT THE RIGHT MEETINGS

The project communicator should, as already discussed, be on the project or programme board. This gives a good opportunity to understand the project politics and where the project thinking is going.

It can be easy to spend all day at meetings, so be selective. Review the terms of reference (TOR), action logs and minutes for each meeting and make a judgement about whether attendance would be helpful.

FIND OUT HOW THE PROJECT FITS INTO THE WIDER CONTEXT

Where the project is part of a programme and possibly a portfolio, there needs to be an understanding of the overall objectives. There may be opportunities to do joined-up communication and messaging which is good practice. It can also help to avoid any clashes of communication.

Having gained a good understanding of the project it is important to keep up to date with changes. There should be a process in place for managing any changes to the project – usually known as 'change control'. Communicators need to make sure that they are involved in this process – many changes will be insignificant from a communication perspective but some will impact on planned communication and significant changes may need to be supported with a communication plan.

Building Effective Relationships

The successful project communicator is a good networker and builds effective working relationships within the project, across the wider organisation of which the project is a part and sometimes externally. There are three main purposes of these relationships:

- Inputs: the knowledge needed to design the communication strategy, messages and plan.

- Client management: the project communicator provides support, content and/or communication materials to another part of the project.

- Supportive: sometimes it will be necessary to ask for support from others on the project or outside it in order to achieve a required outcome.

In Table 1.6, a guide is given to some of the likely key relationships and the outcomes that the project communicator should seek from them. Often a relationship will provide inputs into communication and also be a client of communication. The relationships will vary according to the nature of the project.

Table 1.6   Key relationships for the project communicator and expected outcomes

Relationship	Purpose of the relationship from a communication perspective
Design team (those that are designing what the project will ultimately deliver, for example an IT system)	Input: to gain an understanding of the solution that the project will deliver. Client: ensures the project vision is communicated throughout this phase and that participants from outside the project understand their role in the design.
Project management office (PMO)	Input: the PMO can help with understanding of the project plan and ensure communication activity is aligned.
Project manager	Input: strategic direction. Client: the communication function is there to help the project reach its milestones and deliver its benefits. It also supports and advises the project manager on team leadership and stakeholder communication.
Business change	Input: understanding the scale of the change. Client: supports the business change activity.
Training	Input: training needs analysis may identify things that can be addressed through communication rather than training. Client: helps to ensure that training delegates have reached a sufficient level of awareness before entering training.
Transition	Input: explains how transition from one way of working to another will be managed. Client: specific communication plans and materials to support cutover.
Corporate communication, including press office, design team, internal communication, stakeholder management, public affairs in the wider organisation	Client: messages and communication plans are aligned across the wider organisation. Supportive: central communication teams can provide support and advice. Share ideas and best practice.
Communicators in other projects	Supportive: opportunities to join up messages and check that plans don't conflict. Share ideas and best practice. Client: where there are dependencies, other projects may also be stakeholders.
HR	Client: where the project is changing, creating or removing roles, communication plans need to be aligned with HR plans and in line with policy.
Within government, political leaders' offices	Client: alerting to potential political implications of project activity.
Supplier/partner communication teams	Input: align plans and messages. There may be a requirement to approve supplier/partner communication materials.

Personal Stakeholder Relationships

It is important for the project communicator to identify his or her own personal stakeholders and to be proactive, engaging with them on a regular basis. This should involve giving visibility to the communication activity, something which can get forgotten when the communicator is busy getting on with the job in hand.

Visibility of the communication function is important because it enables the communicator to have influence within the project and be brought into discussions at the right time which all helps with the development of successful strategies. If people are unsure what the communication function is doing, they are less likely to want to engage with it.

Setting communication objectives and measuring against them is an important part of this, but of equal importance is ensuring that the right people know that this is happening. It can be beneficial for the project communicator to carry out an analysis of his or her own personal stakeholders and put a plan in place to ensure that there is understanding of the communication role and what it is achieving for the project.

Communication's own stakeholders will be within the project of course but also beyond it, they can include:

- project sponsor/SRO;

- project board members;

- work stream leads;

- communication colleagues in a central corporate communication function;

- communication colleagues on other projects;

- functional directors (where not already part of the project board), for example HR, Finance and Procurement.

Where the project is part of a programme and possibly a portfolio, additional layers of stakeholders will be in place. These are important working relationships but should also be treated as stakeholders rather than as simply functional. As a general principle the project communicator should think in terms of spending 80 per cent of time on delivering project communication and the remaining 20 per cent ensuring that this is visible. This isn't vanity, rather it is an essential aspect of the role that will help to ensure that the function is taken seriously and thus enable better communication solutions to be delivered. Visibility simply means ensuring the stakeholders who have been identified understand the strategy, what communication activity is being undertaken and the results achieved.

BEING A LONE COMMUNICATOR

Very often the project requirements are such that only a single communication role is required. It can be quite isolating to be a lone communicator when everyone else on the project shares a skill set with those around them or have roles that are often understood much more clearly than that of communication. If these are the circumstances, then the communicator should think about building relationships outside the project with fellow communicators. These relationships will be beneficial in terms of sharing ideas or seeking a best practice solution to a communication problem. Developing and maintaining a communication network will provide support for the communicator and lead to more effective outcomes for the project.

Summary

This chapter has looked at the things to consider when setting up a project communication function including scoping the communication requirement and being clear about what communication is and isn't there to do. It has highlighted that communication is both a strategic and technical function that works best when it has a voice at the project board. With the right skills and competencies at the right level, the communication function is then well placed to develop an effective communication strategy that supports the realisation of project benefits.

2

Developing the Strategy

Failing to plan is planning to fail – or so the saying goes. It can be easy to claim that there isn't enough time to plan but this becomes a vicious circle; without taking time to plan, effort is unfocussed and more likely to be ineffective. Time and energy is wasted on scatter-gun activity. It is important to break this cycle and spend time on strategic planning. This doesn't have to be onerous or take a lot of time. It is actually a very simple process and a rewarding one to go through. It is also a good opportunity to involve project team colleagues and stakeholders which helps to gain buy-in for the communication activity as well as find out more about project work stream plans and activity.

This chapter explains the role of the communication strategy then goes through the strategic planning process step by step and covers:

- understanding the situation;

- identifying stakeholders;

- aims and objectives;

- messaging;

- deciding on the best strategic approach;

- developing the plan and tactics;

- evaluation (throughout – not just at the end).

Some elements of a communication strategy (including stakeholder analysis and evaluation) are discussed in more depth in later chapters. The focus here is on the strategic planning process and the structure of the communication strategy document. The communication strategy document itself will contain sections on all of the above and some additional headings. A template can be found on page 42 as part of the Project Communicator's Toolkit.

Strategic Planning and the Role of the Communication Strategy

Strategic planning means carrying out research and analysis of the situation before deciding what to do. It is a step-by-step process with one stage informing the next. A model for strategic planning can be found in Figure 2.1. A communication plan that simply shows what is going to be done by when without a strategy behind it isn't a plan; it is just a calendar of activity. Strategic planning:

- is based on research;

- is supportive of the project goals and milestones;

- reflects the project vision;

- supports delivery of benefits;

- is intelligent – drawing on communication theory;

- is results based – objectives are measurable, and measured.

The term strategy is generally taken to mean the solution that moves something from A to B. A plan is how this is going to be done. For example, a company may decide that it will achieve growth by developing a new product; this would be its strategy for growth. A plan would then be drawn up that details how this is going to be achieved, for example market research, new product development, product testing and promotion. Or on a more personal level, imagine that the objective is to get a promotion; the strategy could be to become better qualified and the tactic would be to go on a training course. In communication terms it is much the same. A communication strategy explains how objectives are to be met through communication activity, but it doesn't go into the detail of what will actually be done when – this goes into the plan.

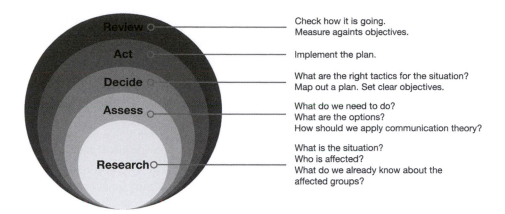

Figure 2.1   The RADAR model of planning
Source: *Exploring Public Relations,* Ruck (2012), © Simon & Schuster Europe Limited 1998, © Pearson Education Limited 2002, 2008.

The communication strategy guides the delivery of all communication activity. Sign-off of the strategy should be at the highest level within the project. Ideally it should be presented at the project board with members taken through each stage. (It can be helpful to 'socialise' the strategy before hand with colleagues and stakeholders so that there are no surprises once at the board table. This is a good way to increase buy-in to the strategy.)

This visibility and buy-in matters because it can seem as though everyone is an expert when it comes to communication and the project communicator can feel pressured into a course of action that may not be appropriate. When a well thought through strategy based on research is in place that has been created along with colleagues and is supported by the project leadership this is less likely to happen and if it does, polite reference back to the agreed strategy can be an effective way of explaining why an idea won't be taken forward.

The communication strategy also acts as a business case in that it sets out the best approach to communication with costs attached. A well constructed and well argued communication strategy is more likely to achieve the funding necessary to deliver quality communication.

Once produced and signed off, the strategy will need to be reviewed on a regular basis to reflect any changes in the project, for example timescales or changes in scope. It also makes sense to limit the scope of the strategy document in terms of time. Over the lifetime of a project, the strategy may need to change quite radically and rather than try to capture this in one document at the outset, it can make more sense to update the approach during the project lifecycle. This will need to be explained in the scope section and the review and revision process outlined. Quarterly reviews are usually sufficient with perhaps a more fundamental revision at key project lifecycle stages being necessary.

All communication activity will be addressing the needs of stakeholders and the strategy document should capture information about them. For this reason, the strategy document itself can be referred to as the 'communication and stakeholder engagement strategy'. In some project methodologies, this is the required title.

Step One: Understanding the Situation

The first step is to understand the situation that is to be addressed through the communication activity. The research that is done at this stage is referred to as 'input research'. There is more on research in Chapter 7. The situation will of course vary from project to project, but the type of understanding needed to inform the situation may include:

- Project objectives and milestones: it goes without saying that the first step is to understand what the project is setting out to do and by when. The strategy needs to demonstrate how communication will support the delivery of project objectives and reflect project timescales.

- The extent and nature of the change: at the early stages of a project, this may not have been analysed and some assumptions will need to be made. This work is often the remit of the business change function but there may be a need to make those assumptions before this team is in place. This is an important step because the level of communication input required will depend on the extent of the change. Project team members can overestimate the extent of the change and it is important to remember that there isn't necessarily a correlation between the complexity or cost of a project and the degree of change.

- Existing levels of stakeholder awareness, understanding and stakeholder perceptions: this is where some research can be useful. The next step will be to set communication objectives which should be measurable so benchmarking will be needed in order to know the current levels of awareness and understanding so that any increase can be measured. It will also highlight at an early stage any concerns among stakeholders and risks that may need to be raised. This exercise is just as important to do within the project team to gauge the level of understanding of the vision for example. In the early stages of the project, it will not be surprising to find that the vision isn't widely understood by all stakeholders, but the project team should be clear from the outset. If this isn't the case, then this is something that will need to be addressed as a priority.

- The organisational culture: culture can be difficult to understand, but can have an impact on the way that communications are received. Different organisations or parts of organisations have different communication preferences – try to understand them. Find out what type of communication has worked well in the past. There is more about culture in the Vignette at the end of this chapter,

- The organisation's ability to adapt to change or its readiness for change: even the most adaptable organisation may groan at the prospect of another project coming along to change the way that it works. If there is a lot of change taking place, establish where this project sits in terms of priority, this will influence the share of voice that the project is likely to achieve.

- Risks and issues: the project risks and issues register should be reviewed. There may be risks that communication can help to mitigate. There may also be a need to build confidence in the project or explain what is being done to address any issues that have already arisen.

- Lessons learned from previous projects: these logs can be extremely helpful in avoiding mistakes but also for finding out what works well. They can provide an insight into the culture of the organisation too. However, they should also be treated with some caution, check who prepared them and what the process was. It is important to ensure that they weren't drafted in order to present a previous project in a good light rather than give an honest account of how things ran.

- Budget: it can be helpful to know what budget might be available for communication before setting out the strategy – for example, a strategy based on lots of local face-to-face activity may not be feasible if budgets are tight. Having said that, it is important to make the case for additional funding if it is felt strongly that a particular communication approach is needed and a well thought through strategy can be a vehicle for doing this.

IDENTIFYING COMMUNICATION PROBLEMS

Throughout the life of a project there are certain to be times when a problem arises and a communication solution is called for. When there is a problem to solve, two things often happen in communication:

- rather than being brought the problem, the communication team is brought the solution;

- the wrong problem is presented.

Whichever happens, the important thing here is for everyone to stop and check that they have identified the right problem. Of course this can be difficult when a more senior colleague – the project manager or sponsor – is demanding that a poster campaign is in place by the end of the week, but it is time well spent and means that the strategic approach chosen is more likely to be effective. Table 2.1 gives some examples of problem misdiagnosis and inappropriate solutions.

There are many different approaches to problem identification, but the simplest way is to make enquiries of those who know about the issue in order to understand it better. It is often the case that the problem as finally identified will be quite different to the one first presented. Without this enquiry, resources can be wasted on an approach and tactics that are never going to resolve the problem.

A technique for doing this is creative problem solving. Ruck (2012) suggests the following group activity:

1. The problem owner presents problem and context and writes the summary on a flipchart using words like "how can I or we…"

2. Questions are then asked for clarification – BUT avoid offering solutions or making judgments at this stage.

3. The problem owner answers questions factually, avoiding justifications or defensive statements.

4. After a period of questioning, the group individually writes down their own definition of problem using "how can I or we…"

5. Each definition is written up on flipchart.

6. The problem owner chooses or re-creates a final version.

Table 2.1   The communication function is often brought the solution rather than the problem and often the problem is misdiagnosed

Original problem/solution as presented	Actual problem and solution
'We need to organise a team building event for our suppliers.'	There is some mistrust and poor communication between suppliers. After further enquiries, it is established that this is because their relationship is not adequately defined in their contracts. A team building event would not solve this problem. It is not a communication problem and needs to be resolved by the procurement function.
'The project intranet isn't being used – we need to tell people to use it.'	The actual problem is that the intranet isn't kept up to date and people find out what is happening more quickly from their colleagues. The solution may be to keep the intranet up to date or it may be that there isn't a need for a project intranet because other channels are more effective.
'We need a poster campaign to explain our ways of working to our colleagues overseas.'	The perceived problem was that project team members in another country did not understand the expected ways of working and it was felt that a poster campaign explaining was the answer. The actual problem was that nobody had ever taken the time to explain the ways of working expected of this team or considered cultural differences. A poster campaign is a one-way form of communication and as such will not result in the level of behaviour change required.

Step Two: Identifying Stakeholders

This aspect of the strategy is discussed in more detail in Chapter 3. The communication strategy should explain who the project will engage with. This piece of work needs to be done early on in the strategic planning process and forms part of the analysis stage. An understanding of stakeholder perspectives will feed into the communication objectives and messaging.

Step Three: Aims and Objectives

The aim (or goal) of the communication strategy is overarching and more general than an objective. It doesn't carry measures in the same way as an objective, but still needs to be clear and easy to understand. It steers the direction the strategy should take and must be underpinned by measureable objectives. For example, the aim or goal of the strategy may be to:

- 'Help ensure a smooth transition to the new ways of working,' or

- 'Obtain stakeholder support for the project.'

This leads into objective setting. Objectives must support the aim or goal of the strategy and are important because they:

- give focus and direction;

- enable activities to be measured effectively;

- ensure best use is made of resources;

- encourage project leaders and stakeholder to buy in to the communication approach;

- help the most appropriate tactics to be selected.

In addition, project communication objectives should:

- support project objectives and milestones;

- be communication related.

Setting objectives that are purely communication related can be harder than it sounds. For example, 'achieving sign-off for the design of the new system' would not be entirely within the gift of the communication function to deliver, but it may be a project-level aim or objective and can be supported through communication, for an example see Table 2.2. It is important to spend time getting the communication objectives right as these are how the success of the strategy should be judged.

Table 2.2   Project level and communication level objectives

Project level objective	Example of supporting communication objective
Achieve sign-off of the new system design by the end of the financial year.	Ensure that all stakeholders involved in the design are clear about the process for feedback by the end of the month.

HOW TO WRITE A GOOD COMMUNICATION OBJECTIVE

The principle of SMART objectives is well established and remains highly relevant for communication. A SMART objective is:

- Specific

- Measurable

- Achievable

- Relevant

- Timed

A SMART objective is specific leaving no room for doubt about what is intended. In project communication terms this usually means specifying who will be communicated with and exactly what they need to know, think or do. Always ensure that the objectives set are achievable, otherwise the strategy may be set to fail from the outset. Examples of a poorly worded objective compared to a SMART objective is given in Table 2.3.

Table 2.3   The difference between poorly worded and SMART objectives

Poorly worded objective	'To raise awareness of the project.'	This objective does not explain who needs to be aware or by when. There is no measure – what is the increase required? Who needs to be aware? It should say how many people and give a date by when a level of awareness should be reached.
SMART objective	'60% of finance staff to be aware of the project vision by the end of the calendar year.'	This objective sets out who is to be communicated with, it contains a measure and a timescale.

Providing SMART objectives is another good way to get the project leadership to engage with the communication strategy. The project board needs to be involved in their development and agree them. Then there has to be regular reporting against them. This visibility and engagement with the objectives is important, because it is another way of ensuring that the communication effort stays focussed. Any shift in the communication requirement should be discussed in light of objectives already set and agreed.

TYPES OF OBJECTIVES

An important distinction for communication objectives is the difference between outcomes and outputs.

- Output: about what has been done.

- Outcome: about what has been achieved.

Examples are given in Table 2.4. Output objectives are useful but should not be used in isolation; there is no point knowing how many people clicked on the website if it is not known what they thought or did as a result.

Table 2.4   The difference between output and outcome objectives

Example output objectives	To produce two newsletters a month for the life of the project. To increase unique visitors to the project intranet page by 10% within the next three months.
Outcome objective	80% of attendees at the briefing event agree that they know what the project will mean for them.

Also think of outcome objectives in terms of the type of outcomes required, for example:

- awareness and understanding;

- attitudes – encouraging belief;

- readiness for change;

- behaviour – act in a particular way.

The objectives will change during the life of the project and the communication strategy revised accordingly. During the project initiation phase objectives may be about awareness but as the project moves towards implementation, behaviour change may be required. This will be different according to the stakeholder group. The type of objective will be influenced by the stage in the project lifecycle and stakeholder group (see Figure 2.2). For example, in the early concept stages, the focus will be on sponsors and senior stakeholders and the objectives will be to move them through awareness to commitment and support for the project. For those who will ultimately use the new product or services the change is probably a long way in the distance and it may be too early even for raising awareness. Figure 2.2 provides an illustration of this.

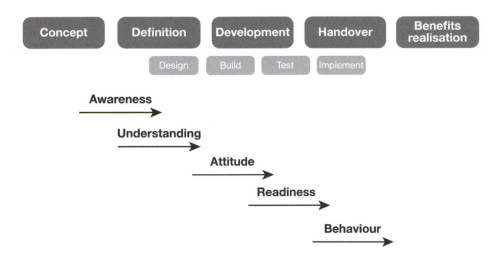

Figure 2.2   **Different types of objectives for those who will use the product or service being developed should be set at different stages of the project lifecycle**

There may be quite a lot of objectives in the strategy document, with different ones being set for different stakeholder groups. There is no right or wrong answer to how many objectives should be contained within the strategy, this will depend on the needs identified during the initial research phase and the overarching aim of the strategy.

Step Four: Deciding the Strategic Approach

Having defined the objectives, the next step is to decide the best strategic approach in order to achieve them; this is one of the most important stages of developing the strategy. The strategic approach is different to the tactics that will be employed as part of the plan. The approach is broader and over arching, whereas the tactics are the individual activities that will be carried out. The key thing is to match the strategic approach to the objectives that have been set.

Different objectives will call for different strategic approaches. For example, if the objective is to change behaviour, then the strategic approach would need to be much more about involving people in the project than simply telling them about the change. In a situation like this where it is clear that the strategic approach should be a programme of two-way communication, then the activity needs to be designed accordingly. Workshops and team discussions where feedback is gathered and taken on board are examples of two-way communication activities. However, a simple one-way communication strategy might be all that is needed if the requirement is to raise awareness or let people know about something straightforward and noncontroversial. Then an intranet story, poster or email may be appropriate.

Consider how the project can contribute to employee engagement. This is a priority for many organisations. Project activity should not undermine engagement and if possible should try to increase it. A strategy based around employee engagement principles would involve ensuring that stakeholders have timely and accurate information about what is happening, have the opportunity to get involved and know that their feedback will be taken on board if possible. There is much more about employee engagement in the Vignette at the end of this chapter.

When the project is bringing about change, the strategic approach should also take into account where stakeholders are on the change curve. A common error on projects is to try and 'sell' the change too early. No amount of 'sell' messaging will make people think positively about the project if there are underlying concerns, for example about jobs, that haven't been addressed. The change curve was invented by Elisabeth Kübler-Ross in the 1960s to illustrate how people deal with the news that they have a terminal illness. It has been adapted and developed to explain how people deal with change in other areas of their life, particularly work. Figure 2.3 sets out how the busiest stages of the project lifecycle from a communication perspective (development, handover and benefits realisation) map to the change curve.

When stakeholders are in denial about the changes to come or are resistant to them, a strategy that pushes out 'sell' messages is likely to increase these behaviours. Instead, stakeholders need to be involved and help to shape the outcome of the project. Of course different stakeholders will go through the change curve at different times. Sponsors and senior stakeholders who have been involved from the start will be enthusiastic and committed before others are even aware of the project. This means that the strategic approach for each group must be different according to the stage of the project lifecycle.

As the project moves into implementation, the most appropriate strategic approach may be to focus on simple, accessible directional messages that explain to people what they need to do differently. An element of two-way dialogue will still be needed of course, responding to feedback during the implementation phase can help to identify and address any unforeseen problems and help to ensure that benefits are realised. There is more about channels and tactics in Chapter 5.

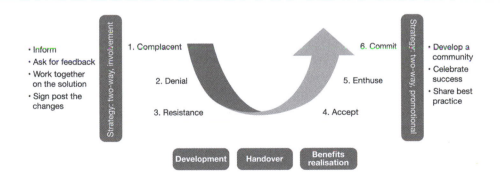

Figure 2.3   The change curve, project lifecycle and strategic communication approaches

Note: Remember that different stakeholders will go through the change curve at different stages in the project lifecycle.

Step Five: Messaging

Having an agreed set of messages is important to ensure consistency across all project communication. Developing and discussing the messages can often be a useful exercise in itself because it will expose whether there are different levels of understanding within the project. If there are, this will of course need to be addressed perhaps by the project manager or senior sponsor. If there isn't a consistent understanding within the project team then the chances of stakeholders being clear about what is happening is unlikely.

Key project messages should be reinforced throughout all communication activity. They may not be the main reason for a communication, but every opportunity should be taken to remind stakeholders of them.

It is likely that throughout the life of the project there will be the need for new messages to be developed – sometimes rapidly – as things change or queries arise that had not been anticipated. Only fundamental changes to messaging need to be included in the strategy, a simple 'frequently asked question' document is often all that is needed to capture messages that are in effect answers to questions.

The communication messages can be factual or designed to bring about a change in attitude or behaviour. Factual messages will be statements about the project that aim to answer some of the key questions that stakeholders may have and address some of the areas where there is the potential for ambiguity. Messages in the strategy may, for example, set out the rationale for the programme, the benefits that are expected and any key design principles.

Messages can also be used to influence attitudes to the project. These messages will need to be tailored to different stakeholders because they need to be designed to address the particular needs of that group. For example, if a change of behaviour is needed then messages should set out to address what is blocking that behaviour change. This relies on an understanding of the stakeholder so some research may be necessary to ensure that the message is appropriate. Of course, it is important to realise that simply delivering a message, however well thought through, will not in itself be enough to change behaviour, this is best achieved through two-way communication involving discussion and willingness by both parties to be flexible and adapt.

Messages should be simple and straightforward in language and tone. They do not necessarily always have to be communicated verbatim, it should be possible for anyone on the project to understand and communicate them.

Think about incorporating the messages into a 'narrative' or story rather than – or as well as – presenting them as a list of bullet points. This can make communication easier and helps people put things into their own words, while still staying true to the project messages. This approach can be particularly useful when setting the project messages in the context of wider corporate messages enabling one, joined-up story to be told.

The following factors should be taken into account when developing messages:

- the objective that they are designed to help deliver;

- the type of message required, for example is it to raise awareness or perhaps to persuade someone to change their behaviour;

- the current views of the stakeholder who will be targeted with the message;

- the needs of the stakeholder – what does he or she want to know? If there are outstanding questions, these can act as 'noise' until resolved and prevent other messages being heard.

There is more about messaging and how to tell the project story in Chapter 4.

Step Six: Develop the Plan and Tactics

As discussed in step five above, the objectives dictate the strategic approach and the strategic approach guides which communication channels and tactics will be best to use. Channels and tactics are discussed in detail in Chapter 5. Chapter 6 deals with how to build the communication plan.

Step Seven: Evaluate

This chapter has discussed the importance of research as an input to strategic communication planning but research is also used throughout the implementation of the strategy to check if it is working. If it isn't, then the approach can be adjusted and different tactics designed. Chapter 7 equips project communicators with the knowledge needed to conduct or commission research.

Summary

This chapter has explained the strategic planning process and focussed in detail on understanding the situation, objective setting and selection of the right strategic approach. Strategic planning is a step-by-step process with each stage informing the next and only when this is complete should the actual communication activities be designed. The result of the strategic planning process is set out in the communication strategy document. A template follows as part of the Project Communicator's Toolkit.

Project Communicator's Toolkit: Communication and Stakeholder Engagement Strategy Document Template

REQUIRED PROJECT INFORMATION

The communication strategy should be formatted in line with other project documentation. This may include a change history, review dates, author details, plus who is authorised to sign-off or make changes. If in any doubt, work with the PMO.

The communication function should champion adherence to house style and branding guidelines so it is important to ensure that all communication documentation is compliant.

INTRODUCTION AND BACKGROUND

Set the scene for the reader. Explain the context in which the communication strategy has been developed. This need only be a couple of paragraphs but is helpful in ensuring that everyone who reads or reviews the document has the same understanding of the context.

SCOPE

What will and won't be addressed through the strategy? If it is a programme-level communication strategy be clear about whether all the projects are included – or do they have their own strategies and plans? Will the strategy last for the lifetime of the project or is it addressing a particular phase?

This section also provides a good opportunity to remind project leaders and stakeholders what communication is not there to do, for example set out the tasks that are the role of others such as the project/programme management office or external media relations (which may sit with a central press office function for example).

PROGRAMME RELATIONSHIP

If the project is part of a programme then it is good practice to explain how the project strategy will be aligned with programme-level activity. Will the programme govern project communication? If so, how will this work?

ROLES AND RESPONSIBILITIES

Outline who is responsible for what (see the discussion on this in Chapter 1).

STAKEHOLDERS

This is where the stakeholder analysis work should be captured. Explain who the stakeholders are, how they are being prioritised, engaged and tracked. Remember that stakeholders may well be involved in the review and sign-off of the strategy and so will read this analysis.

AIMS AND COMMUNICATION OBJECTIVES

Give the objectives of the communication strategy here. These should be SMART, that is, specific, measurable, achievable, relevant and time-bound. It is important that these objectives are agreed by the programme or project board. Evaluation should be carried out against these objectives in order to judge the success of the communication strategy.

There will be a number of objectives, possibly a different set for each stakeholder group, and these will change over the life of the project. Make it clear what phase of the project the objectives relate to.

STRATEGIC APPROACH

Explain the strategic approach here. For example is this a campaign that simply needs to 'tell' stakeholders something or does it require a co-creation approach with stakeholders contributing to the debate and shaping the decisions? It might be that different approaches are adopted at different stages during the lifecycle of the programme and that journey can be detailed here (in line with the scope already set out above).

KEY MESSAGES

List the key messages to be delivered by the communications here. Messages will be different according to the stakeholder or audience group. They should be designed to deliver the communication objectives. If there is a story or 'narrative' about the project, include it here.

As well as high-level messages – for example, why a change is happening – there may be 'instructional' messages too. For example: 'Book your training by the end of the month.'

It can be helpful to make reference here to wider corporate messages where appropriate. This helps to set the project in the context of other things that are happening in the organisation or in the environment in which the project exists. This is good practice and helps stakeholders to understand how the project fits together with other initiatives.

CHANNELS

Talk here about what channels will be used to deliver the communication strategy. Keep this at the strategic level. For example, will existing trusted channels be used or will new channels need to be created? Will the focus be on electronic communication, social media, face-to-face events or a mix of both? Explain what type of messages each channel will be used for. For example, important news announcements may be sent by email but more general project updates may fit better into a regular, weekly communication bulletin. This is known as the 'channel management strategy'.

MEDIA RELATIONS

This section may or may not be needed depending on the nature of the project. If the project is largely external facing, then the whole strategy will reflect the need to work with the media. However, even when the project is mostly internal there will still be the potential for media interest. Jobs being lost or moved, premises closed or large sums being spent on IT systems in the public sector are just some examples of potential media stories. Explain here who will handle the media and who – if anyone – has the authority to speak to them. It may not all be negative though, there may be a good story to tell, but protocols still need to be in place to ensure it is managed appropriately.

RISKS AND DEPENDENCIES

Risks and issues should be captured and tracked within the appropriate risk register and that can be explained here. In addition, highlight any dependencies for the successful delivery of the strategy. This might include budget or other resource.

RESOURCES AND BUDGET

Identify who will be involved in managing and delivering the communication plan that delivers the strategy, outlining the estimated time involved for in-house people. Any additional external support required should also be clearly set out with full costs provided. Explain who is responsible for reviewing and updating the strategy document.

SIGN-OFF PROTOCOLS

Set out how communication messages and products will be signed off; who is involved and who has the final approval. Add in agreed turnaround times so everyone knows how quickly they need to do things.

EVALUATION

Explain how the strategy will be evaluated. This should be against the objectives that have been set and agreed. Evaluation should happen at intervals throughout the delivery of the strategy so that if something isn't working, this can be identified early and adjusted. This evaluation should feed into regular reports to the project board. The method of evaluation for each objective should be set out. This may include hits to an intranet or website, interviews with stakeholders, a survey and post-event evaluation sheets.

REPORTING

Set out how and when performance against the strategy will be reported.

Vignette: Employee Engagement

Employee engagement is of increasing importance to many organisations with initiatives being introduced to increase engagement and measurement put in place to see if they are working. But what is this thing called 'engagement' and why is it important for project communication?

In 2009, the UK Government commissioned a report on the topic: Engaging for Success, authored by David MacLeod and Nita Clarke. They describe engagement as a workplace approach designed to ensure that employees are committed to their organisation's goals and values, motivated to contribute to organisational success, and are able at the same time to enhance their own sense of well-being. The study showed the link between levels of engagement and organisational performance as well as being associated with improved feelings of well-being among employees.

An understanding of employee engagement matters for project communication because:

- When the project is part of a wider organisation, it should ensure that as far as possible, implementation will not impact negatively on engagement levels within that organisation and where possible, contribute to increased levels.

- An engaged project team is more likely to deliver successful project outcomes.

So, how is engagement achieved and what has it got to do with communication? The Engaging for Success report identified four main drivers for engagement:

- Leadership: there is a strong strategic narrative which has widespread ownership and commitment from managers and employees at all levels. The narrative is a clearly expressed story about what the purpose of an organisation is, why it has the broad vision it has and how an individual contributes to that purpose.

- Engaging managers: are at the heart of this organisational culture – they facilitate and empower rather than control or restrict their staff; they treat their staff with appreciation and respect and show commitment to developing, increasing and rewarding the capabilities of those they manage.

- Voice: employees' views are sought out; they are listened to and see that their opinions count and make a difference. They speak out and challenge when appropriate.

- Integrity: behaviour throughout the organisation is consistent with stated values, leading to trust and a sense of integrity.

The project communicator can and should influence all of the above within the project, although he or she will can have more influence on some factors than on others. Table 2.5 suggests how project communicators can contribute to the drivers of engagement and where they are likely to have most impact.

Table 2.5   How project communication can contribute to the drivers of engagement

Engagement driver	Role of project communicator	Degree of influence for project communication
Voice	<ul><li>Providing timely and accurately information about what is happening.</li><li>Facilitating gathering feedback and responding to it.</li><li>Introducing channels that enable an informed employee voice.</li></ul>	High
Leadership	<ul><li>Facilitating collaboration in development of the project vision.</li><li>Ensuring vision is simple and easy to understand.</li><li>Supporting project leadership team in communicating the project vision and reminding them to do so.</li><li>Ensuring vision is reiterated as part of ongoing communications.</li><li>Developing the project story or 'narrative'.</li></ul>	High
Engaging managers	<ul><li>Helping to establish structures for reward and recognition within the team.</li><li>Visibility of reward and appreciation of team efforts.</li></ul>	Medium
Integrity	<ul><li>Acting as a critical friend with the project leadership team to highlight when actions aren't in line with the vision and organisational values.</li></ul>	Medium

Informed Employee Voice

Giving employees a voice is the area where project communicators can perhaps have the most influence and it could be argued that this has the greatest impact on engagement. If stakeholders feel that they have a say in what happens and that they are listened to then they are more likely to feel committed to the project, see Fig. 2.4. The rule applies to both project team members and stakeholders.

The good news is that projects often have governance processes in place that enable stakeholders to help shape solutions, for example through conference room pilots, membership of boards and so on.

However, for employee voice to be effective two other things must be in place:

- information;

- action.

INFORMED EMPLOYEE VOICE: INFORMATION

People need to understand what it is that they are being asked to have an opinion on before they are able to make a contribution. It can sometimes seem that staff aren't interested in what is happening on the project or in the organisation and don't take the opportunity to get involved – they just want to come to work, do their job and go

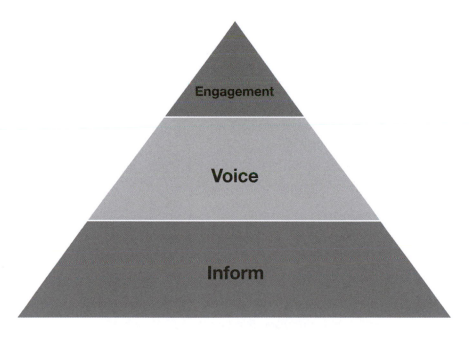

Figure 2.4   **Engagement results from providing accurate, timely information and giving employees a voice**

home. But this may be because they don't feel able to contribute because they don't have the information they need to enable them to make a meaningful contribution. Or it could be because there is a history of voices being sought out, but then ignored.

Information needs to be honest, accurate and timely. The project must avoid slipping into propaganda at all costs – everyone will see through this. It is a mistake to think that simply telling everyone that things are great will make it so. Nothing undermines credibility more quickly and the result will be cynicism and disengagement. When communicating on projects this can be a challenge. Project leadership teams are often passionate about what they are implementing and can forget that colleagues and stakeholders may not have the same level of understanding or have personal concerns about the impact of the project. Their views may be influenced by previous projects that have failed to deliver, fear about jobs, or concern for the environment. When informing about the project, it is important to think about what the project team member or stakeholder would want to know, remembering that this may be very different from what the project leadership team might think they need to know.

This must be identified through the communication planning process. The different stakeholders (individuals and groups) within the project and outside it must be identified and their communication requirements – that is, what matters to them – being captured.

Information requirements may include:

- project vision;

- timescales/roadmap;

- decision making process;

- decisions made;

- dependencies;

- the benefits case;

- impact on jobs;

- what individuals or teams may have to do differently;

- external influences (for example, political, financial).

Keeping people informed can be achieved through largely one-way communication but it can be helpful if there is also an opportunity to discuss messages in order to check understanding. A combination of one-way communication channels (for example, newsletters and intranets) supported by discussion in team or stakeholder meetings is best.

INFORMED EMPLOYEE VOICE: ACTION

Once a level of understanding has been reached, employees can make effective use of the voice given to them. Giving employees a voice comes with responsibility to listen and act where possible. It doesn't mean that a project will have to do everything that is suggested, but it does mean being willing to involve team members and stakeholders and allowing them to shape the solution, business implementation approach and so on. If an idea comes forward that simply isn't do-able that's fine, just explain why. It is this final step that is often missed, leaving people feeling ignored and undervalued.

If previous projects have listened but failed to take any action or to close the feedback loop, then it is likely that attempts to do so on a new project will be met with cynicism. People may be reluctant to get involved bringing a risk that important insights will be lost to the project. It can take time to build trust where none exists, but it is time well spent.

The role of the project communicator here is to ensure that there are structures in place to gather feedback and keep stakeholders updated on action that has been taken. This responsibility is outside the project governance structures where feedback may be being gathered as part of activities such as conference room pilots. This activity should be managed by the appropriate work stream/project team although communication can be used to keep those stakeholders who aren't involved up to date with what has been suggested and decided.

This process of listening to stakeholders and aiming for mutual understanding is true two-way communication and is a major contributor to engagement. It involves not only the project leadership being willing to listen and adapt but also team members and stakeholders being willing to do the same. The aim is for a balanced relationship. Mechanisms for two-way communication may include:

- workshops;

- team meetings;

- focus groups;

- one-to-one meetings.

Challenges in an Engagement Approach to Project Communication

The idea that the project will have to do what people ask can be a blocker to implementing a truly two-way approach to communication and therefore engagement. Project leaders can feel that once they have opened the door to such a dialogue, an expectation will be raised that can't always be met and, understandably, this can feel like a very negative thing to do. There is always the potential for a stakeholder to feel disappointed if what he or she has suggested can't be implemented, but the project should look to achieve a level of mutual understanding with the stakeholder by providing a rationale for the ultimate decision. Coaching may be needed to get project leaders and managers comfortable with facilitating conversations that will certainly involve having to reject ideas and explaining the reasons why.

Team leaders can help the process by facilitating two-way communication with their teams, gathering feedback to be fed into the project. However, all too often managers think that their role is to 'sell' an idea or a change to their team. Managers will naturally feel reluctant to 'sell' in case things don't work out as planned or perhaps because they genuinely don't see a direct benefit for members of their team. But take away the idea that they have to sell the change and instead ask them to facilitate the conversation and there is more chance of getting them on board to help with the communication.

Knowing When Engagement Has Been Achieved

To know when engagement has been achieved relies on being able to define it in the first place. The Macleod and Clarke definition provided earlier provides a starting point, it talked about engagement being:

- commitment to goals and values;

- motivation to contribute to organisational success;

- an enhanced sense of own well-being.

Many organisations carry out large-scale employee engagement surveys to come up with an engagement score for different parts of the business (the starting point may or may not be the definition above).

In terms of engagement within a project team, this may be captured as part of a wider organisational survey, but sometimes it can be judged simply by the mood of the team. The problem with large-scale surveys is that they can become more about the survey and getting the completion rate up than providing an understanding of engagement levels.

Project communication has much to learn from employee engagement theory. By adopting the principles of keeping stakeholders informed and giving them a voice, not only can engagement levels be maintained or increased but the project has more chance of realising its benefits.

Vignette: Culture

Culture. If only it could be harnessed, shaped and controlled, organisations would work perfectly. Wouldn't they? A happy, productive workforce all pulling in the same direction with shared values and commitment – the project is bound to succeed!

Culture from a project communication perspective can be looked at in two ways:

- as something that can be created and shaped towards an ideal;

- as a way of understanding organisations and people.

Culture as a way of understanding an organisation is a crucial perspective for the communicator. Every communicator will have had the experience of a seemingly well thought through communication failing to achieve the desired result or not being understood in the way that was intended. Very often the recipients of the message will be blamed for not taking the message on board, but is it right to blame, or is it a failure of the communication to acknowledge the culture of the stakeholder group? Culture is a lens through which people see and interpret messages. When communicators think about culture in this way, it becomes clear why sometimes communication doesn't turn out as intended.

Defining Culture

So what exactly is culture? Culture has numerous meanings. Aside from within organisations, the most popular understanding is probably that of national identity. One might suppose that in an organisational sense, culture is easy to define. Many might describe it very simply as 'the way we do things around here', but to understand the concept of culture in the workplace, it is necessary to dig a little deeper.

Terms that are commonly associated with definitions of culture include 'values', 'behaviours', 'beliefs', 'meaning', 'symbols' and 'shared'. Of course there are many more, but this begins to give a flavour of the way culture is typically defined. The term 'typically' is used because there really is no one agreed definition of culture in an organisational sense.

The lack of an agreed definition all seems rather confusing and surprising given how much attention is paid to culture within organisations by leaders and their communication teams.

The interest in culture in relation to the workplace is relatively new and was seized on by management theorists in the 1980s as offering the answer to business leaders' prayers for an organisation that mirrored the success of the Japanese manufacturing sector, a success that was often attributed to their highly cohesive culture. Peters and Waterman's 1982 book *In Search of Excellence* was extremely successful and can doubtless still be found on many executives' book shelves. It attributed success to 'strong' corporate culture. By 'strong' they meant one where customer service, innovation and quality were key values for members of the organisation, with this leading to success. Subsequently some of those 'excellent' companies have failed to prosper in the way that might have been anticipated. It is interesting to bring this up to date by looking at the problems that have beset the Japanese economy during the 2000s.

The central theme of this school of thought was that culture was something to be shaped and managed, moulding employees into corporate beings at one with the vision and values of the organisation.

But of course, just as the term 'strong culture' can describe an organisation where everyone is working towards the same goal, in the same way and with the same values, one could equally apply the term to an organisation where everybody is indeed pulling in the same direction – it just isn't the direction that management would like!

The risk is that if nobody in academia or at the board table is agreed on what it is – how can it be understood, let alone managed or changed? This is perhaps why to some, culture can seem vague or intangible; a concept that is spoken about in meetings with great confidence, and while everyone nods enthusiastically and agrees that the culture must indeed be changed, nobody is really quite sure what needs to happen next or how to judge when the desired culture – whatever that is – has been attained. Sometimes it can seem a little bit like the fable of the Emperor's New Clothes, where it just takes one person at the table to raise their hand and ask somebody exactly what they mean for it to become apparent that nobody really knows.

As well as being seen as a speedy and sure-fire recipe for success, culture can become a shorthand, easier to say than actually articulating the problems and challenges that the organisation faces and working through how to address them.

Figure 2.5   The cultural web

Source: *Exploring Corporate Strategy* 8th edition, Johnson, Scholes and Whittington (2010),
© Simon & Schuster Europe Limited 1998 © Pearson Education Limited 2002, 2008.

Understanding the Culture

A useful tool that can help to interpret culture is the cultural web (Johnson et al.
2008). This incorporates the idea of stories and symbols as well as factors such as
structure and control systems. It is a model that also helps to illustrate the importance
of communication in the culture forming process. Through the 'stories' part of the
web, Johnson et al. encourage us to think about the stories that are told to new
recruits and which link the present to the history of the organisation. Typically, they
say, these stories will be about successes and disasters, heroes, villains and mavericks
who deviate from the norm. The stories legitimise types of behaviour and let people
know what is important in the organisation.

Culture Change

There is no doubt that culture can be an inhibitor to growth and change. Many
people are wary of change and the ambiguity that often seems to go with it. They
understandably feel happier sticking with what they know and feel comfortable
with. For Johnson et al. this can lead to what they term 'strategic drift'. This occurs

when organisations fail to change as needed in line with their environment. A typical response to the pressure for change might be a level of adaptation, but only within the existing ways of working (the paradigm as identified through the cultural web), a more fundamental change being too much of a step change for people to contemplate.

Culture can impact on a project's ability to introduce even quite small-scale change. It may seem simple enough to ask employees to start using new technology – for example, claiming their expenses online rather than use a paper form. Does culture matter in this scenario? Well, that is exactly the question that the project communicator needs to ask. Colleagues in the organisation may talk about potential blockers to the change being things like a lack of information technology (IT) skills or access to a computer and these are important considerations, but there may be deeper cultural considerations that have developed from past experiences of new technology or changes in expenses policy.

Schein (2004: 329–331) discuses the notion of 'learning anxiety' in the context of cultural change, and says that in being asked to change, people can fear:

- temporary incompetence;

- punishment for incompetence;

- loss of personal identity;

- loss of group membership.

The response to change goes through denial, scape-goating or dodging the change (others should change first) and finally to bargaining. He advocates two key principles for the change leader:

- Survival anxiety or guilt must be greater than the learning anxiety.

- Learning anxiety must be reduced rather than increasing survival anxiety.

For the project communicator charged with helping to bring about culture change, perhaps it is best to describe the task in a different way. Instead of talking about culture, instead ask what the organisation wants to achieve. For example, if someone was to say that the organisation needs to develop a 'customer service culture' what does that actually mean and how will the organisation know when it has one? It may mean that staff sound knowledgeable and helpful on the phone and always call back when they say they will and so on. In terms of knowing when this has been achieved, that may be indicated by what customers say about the organisation, whether they buy more, or any one of a number of other similar measures.

With the problem articulated thus, it becomes easier to see what needs to be done. What it won't be about is putting up a big sign in the staff room saying 'customers first' or press-ganging everyone into an expensive customer role-playing exercise during an away day at a country house hotel (although such tactics do have their place).

Instead there will be a number of things to think about:

- Do colleagues have the knowledge needed to help customers?

- Do they feel supported if they don't know the answer?

- Are the products poor, meaning that customers are usually angry anyway?

- Is the call handling technology up to the job?

- Are teams sufficiently staffed?

Morgan (1997: 126) points out that many discussions of Japanese management ignore the cultural–historical circumstances that allowed Japanese management to flourish and overestimated the ease with which the ways of working could be transplanted from one context to another. This illustrates again the danger of assuming that culture is the 'big idea' that will save the company and can be achieved easily through a 'culture change programme'.

Morgan (1997: 147) discusses this when he talks about culture as a metaphor for organisations and how, since the 1980s, there has been a growing emphasis for leaders on creating appropriate systems of shared meaning that can 'mobilize the efforts of people in pursuit of desired aims and objectives'. But he cautions that culture is a 'living, evolving, self-organizing reality that can be shaped and reshaped but not in an absolute way'.

Culture as a Filter of Messages

So an understanding of culture is key to successful project communication, particularly when an element of culture change is required. Individuals create their own meaning and this is a much more complex process than many communicators, leaders and managers realise. It is frustrating when carefully crafted communications aren't received in the way that is wanted or expected, but for those who understand the role that culture plays, this won't be a surprise. To say that stakeholders 'misinterpreted' or 'misunderstood' a message seems to suggest that it is the stakeholder who is 'at fault' but it can be argued that the responsibility is with the initiator of the message who should endeavour to understand the culture of those with whom he or she is communicating.

3

Who Are Our Stakeholders?

Most texts on project management will highlight the importance of identifying, prioritising and engaging with stakeholders and rightly so. But what does the term stakeholder mean? Who are these people called stakeholders, what is the best way to engage them and what is the role for communication?

Essentially, a stakeholder is a person, group of people or organisation that is affected by what a project is doing, or can affect it. Some people know that they are stakeholders, others may be 'latent', that is, they have an interest but they just don't know it yet.

From this definition, it is clear that all project communication activity will revolve around stakeholders so it is essential that the project knows who its stakeholders are and understands their needs.

However, the term 'stakeholder' is sometimes too broad to be helpful – after all, anyone can have an impact on a project so does that mean that the project needs to engage with everyone who might in some way be connected to or affected by what is being delivered? The good news is no – at least, not all at the same time. The key is to prioritise; decide where to focus effort and resources and at what stage of the project lifecycle.

This chapter discusses the nature of stakeholder relationships and then follows a step-by-step process that will help to ensure that they are engaged appropriately.

Stakeholders – A Communication Perspective

The worst mistake a project can make is to assume that those with whom it needs to engage – be they senior sponsors or the ultimate users of a new product or service – are a homogenous group and adopt a 'one-size-fits-all' approach to communication. In fact they will all have their own concerns to which communication activity needs to be tailored.

Stakeholders matter because they can help or hinder the project. An unhappy stakeholder can be exhausting to deal with and may actively undermine project objectives, so it is far better to engage early. The aim should be mutual respect and understanding, it isn't realistic to expect all stakeholders to support a project 100 per cent. The project should be aiming for a balanced relationship; one where stakeholder views are sought out, heard and taken on board if possible but at the same time stakeholders are also prepared to adapt their position.

Working with stakeholders can be time consuming, because to do it effectively means understanding the perspective of each group or individual, but it is time well spent. Taking a proactive, planned approach and guiding others on the project team to lead on stakeholder relationships will make it less onerous.

Identifying and understanding stakeholders is one of the first tasks for the project communicator; it is knowledge that informs the communication strategy.

Not all projects see stakeholder engagement as the remit of the communication function and sometimes there may be a dedicated stakeholder engagement manager employed. There is no right or wrong model but it is essential that the communication function is at the heart of stakeholder engagement work, even if it doesn't lead on it. While the communicator will not necessarily be the owner of a stakeholder relationship, he or she has an important role to play in facilitation and support.

Communicators can equip relationship owners with the messages and tools necessary to make a success of their relationships and ensure that activity is planned and co-ordinated, helping to build the reputation of the project as one that is well managed. A stakeholder will lose confidence quickly should he or she receive an approach from a project team member on Monday, only to

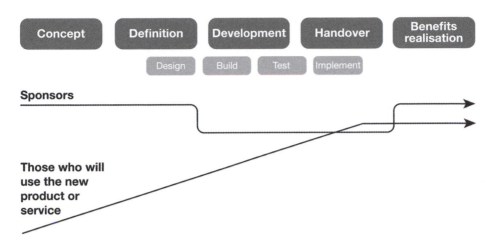

Figure 3.1 The focus of communication activity can shift between stakeholder groups throughout the life of the project

be approached about something different, by someone different, on Tuesday. Simply ensuring that stakeholder contact is planned and co-ordinated can go a long way in securing the reputation of a project.

As the project progresses, the way that communication works with stakeholders will change. In the early days the focus will be on project sponsors with this shifting over the project lifecycle to encompass those who, for example, will use the new product or service. The style of communication will also shift to include more 'broadcast' style communication designed to reach larger groups of people, see Figure 3.1.

Taking a Planned Approach to Stakeholders

Without a planned approach, the stakeholder relationship will be unfocussed and less likely to produce the outcomes desired. Relationship owners should welcome having a structured contact programme in place and support in delivering it. The key steps to planning the stakeholder relationship are:

Step 1: Identify

Step 2: Analyse

Step 3: Decide on the approach

Step 4: Plan

Step 5: Review and update

Step 1: Identify

The first step is to identify who the stakeholders are. The best way to do this is by involving colleagues in the project. Consider running a workshop to capture suggestions, it encourages cross-fertilisation of ideas and will help to secure buy-in across the project to a communication and stakeholder strategy.

However, there needs to be some structure to the exercise to ensure that all the right stakeholders are captured. The stakeholder definition given in the introduction is a starting point (that is, anyone who can affect or is affected by the project), but try using some more specific headings to guide the identification process (see Table 3.1). If the project is taking place within a larger organisation, check if there is an organisational stakeholder strategy – a lot of the thinking might have already been done. There is no point reinventing the wheel and anyway it is important to ensure that project stakeholder engagement activity is joined up with what is happening elsewhere in the organisation of which the project is a part.

The list provided at Table 3.1 isn't exhaustive and some headings won't always be relevant, but think carefully before ruling out a section. For example, the media and politicians may not seem relevant to the project initially, but should something go wrong, could that become visible externally and have a negative impact on the project?

Stakeholders can be captured as individuals or as groups. Take care not to group people together too readily. Check that there isn't someone within that group who is more influential, powerful or interested than others. With this in mind, remember that there is no such thing as the 'general public' or 'all staff'. These groupings are too broad to be useful. Take 'staff' for example, there are directors, line managers and employees who have a particular function (for example, finance or HR). When it comes to the analysis stage it will be clear why this segmentation is important – it is because they will all have different levels of interest and influence.

The list of stakeholders should be included in the project communication and stakeholder engagement strategy.

Table 3.1   Prompts for identifying stakeholders

Internal, within the organisation of which the project is a part	
Identification category	**What to think about**
Those who are funding the project	Ensure that the whole funding chain is considered. The finance director may be directly approving funding, but is there a higher authority? Perhaps a holding company or, in government, another department?
Members of the board of the organisation of which the project is part	Capture members of the board as individuals – some could be more interested than others.
Portfolio, programme and project board members, other members of the governance structure	Again, capture as individuals.
Specialists within the organisation, e.g. procurement, press office, marketing, HR	This will be in addition to functional/working relationships or may overlap with them. Consider whether those at director level are appropriate stakeholders (they probably are) if they aren't already represented within the governance structure.
Employee representative groups	For example trade unions, or other formal staff representatives.
Employees	Employees aren't a homogeneous group, for example line managers and front line staff will have very different needs and concerns.
Project team	
Identification category	**What to think about**
Project leadership team	It can be easy to forget the project colleagues are stakeholders too!
Suppliers and partners	For example, IT or management consultancy providers.
Specialists on whom the project depends	HR, procurement, IT colleagues.
External to the organisation	
Identification category	**What to think about**
Special interest/activist groups	If any of these groups or individuals are identified as stakeholders, ensure that engagement is aligned with anything happens at organisation level and ensure that the relationship owners at this level are sighted on any project activity.
Media	
Politicians (for example, who represent the geographical area where the project is having an impact)	
Local community	

Step 2: Analyse

As mentioned at the start, the danger is that just about everyone can become a stakeholder, but that's fine, the next stage is to analyse and prioritise which will make the engagement appropriate and more manageable.

This process is sometimes known as stakeholder 'mapping'. Again, this is best done with project colleagues. Be careful not to over engineer this process to the extent that it becomes onerous or more about the process than the relationship. The objective here is to work out which stakeholders are most important at a particular time, what their interest is and the best way to engage with them.

There are many models used to help understand stakeholders. External consultancy teams working on the project may have their own preferred methodology or it may be set a programme or portfolio level. A popular methodology is the power/interest matrix. This maps stakeholders according to how much power (or influence) they have and how interested they are in what the project is doing. An example is at Table 3.2.

Table 3.2   Analysing stakeholders: power/interest matrix

	HIGH	Approach: Keep satisfied	Approach: Treat as key players
Power/influence	LOW	Approach: Minimal effort	Approach: Keep informed
		LOW	HIGH

Interest

This is a popular model and will be familiar to many. However, while it is useful in lots of situations, it suggests that less voice is given to those who are interested, but have little influence. Depending what the project is setting out to achieve, this may be inappropriate. For example, some staff groups may be thought to have little influence but is it ethical or helpful not to prioritise them? From an external stakeholder perspective, if the project is designing health services for example, it would be essential – and arguably more ethical – to listen to the voices of those who may use the service but are not thought to have a lot of influence.

It is important to remember too that levels of influence can be hard to judge and do not necessarily equate to grade or status. Wider access to communication channels, particularly through social media, mean that it is increasingly possible for many people to have a voice that possibly leads to influence.

So, the model can be adapted to include a different approach for groups with less influence.

Table 3.3 **Analysing stakeholders, accounting for those with less influence**

Power/influence	HIGH	Keep satisfied	Key players
	LOW	Inform	Consult
		LOW	HIGH

Interest

Doing the initial analysis can take some time but it is important to get it right in order to focus effort appropriately. Once it has been done, schedule regular reviews. Stakeholders will move between the quadrants during the lifecycle of the project and of course people come and go so changes must be captured.

Having prioritised stakeholders in this way, a further step in the analysis is to gauge how supportive they are of the project. Ideally stakeholders will be advocates, but the key word here is 'ideally'. Be realistic, a neutral position may be the best that can be achieved for some.

This analysis can be included in the communication and stakeholder engagement strategy.

ANALYSING STAKEHOLDERS FROM A PROJECT PERSPECTIVE

The analysis tools outlined so far are established methods used in many different contexts. From a project perspective stakeholders can also be considered in terms of their role on the project and their comfort with ambiguity:

- Sponsors: these stakeholders set the direction, hold the budget and can release resources. They are comfortable dealing with a high level of ambiguity.

- Shapers: these stakeholders get involved at the design stage (this could be the design of an IT system, new ways of working or a product). They can see what the future looks like and are relatively comfortable with ambiguity.

- Schedulers: these stakeholders are often 'gatekeepers' they can get things done and make the implementation of the project happen.

- Those who will use the new service, adopt different ways of working and so on (according to what the project is delivering). This group is less comfortable handling ambiguity.

For each group, the project communicator can analyse what is needed from a stakeholder at each stage of the project lifecycle and then design communication activity accordingly. An example is given in Table 3.4.

Step 3: Decide on the approach

Having identified the stakeholders and worked out how important each is at which stage, the next step is to set objectives and to decide how to build a good relationship with them.

The point of the analysis stage is to inform the strategic approach to be taken. It can be easy for a project to view the analysis as a 'tick box' exercise and then simply carry on with a one-size-fits-all approach. As already discussed, the analysis should be a living, working document that is reviewed regularly. If the solution to stakeholder engagement ends up as a newsletter that is sent to everyone on the list, then the analysis either hasn't worked or isn't being used to inform the communication strategy.

SETTING OBJECTIVES FOR THE RELATIONSHIP

Often projects say that they simply want stakeholders' support. However, it is important to understand how this is achieved and agree objectives for the stakeholder activity accordingly. For example, a stakeholder is unlikely to

Table 3.4   Analysing stakeholders, a project perspective

Project phase	Concept	Definition	Development	Handover	Benefits realisation
Role on Project			**Communication task**		
Sponsor Level of comfort with ambiguity: high — Set the direction; Budget and resources	Support the sponsor in developing the vision. Support the sponsor in building commitment to the project. Keep informed to maintain confidence in the project	Support the sponsor in delivering leadership communication to help build the project team. Ensure the sponsor understands and can explain the high-level project plan. Keep informed to maintain confidence in the project	Reinforcing the vision. Supporting the sponsor to help change attitudes. Keep informed to maintain confidence in the project	Support sponsor to be visible to create confidence in the project. Keep informed to maintain confidence in the project	Support sponsor to maintain visibility, talk about the benefits and celebrate success. Ensure the sponsor can acknowledge the impact. Keep informed to maintain confidence in the project
Shapers Level of comfort with ambiguity: medium — Input into the design; Can see the future	Create awareness. Make information available including indicative timescales. Explain how they can get involved and what is expected. Seek and listen to feedback	Communicate the vision and benefits. Explain their role in more detail. Seek and listen to feedback	Provide support so that they can become advocates. Seek and listen to feedback	Provide support so that they can become advocates. Seek and listen to feedback	Ensure the shapers contribution is acknowledged

Table 3.4 Continued

Project phase		Concept	Definition	Development	Handover	Benefits realisation
	Role on Project			Communication task		
Schedulers Level of comfort with ambiguity: medium/low	'Gate keepers' who can get things done	Create early awareness Make information available Signpost future involvement and indicative timescales	Build awareness Make sure information is available Explain likely role and signpost indicative timescales	Keep informed and provide, detail on business impact. Ensure understanding of timescales and what resources will be needed Ensure the scheduler understands what they need to do and by when	Provide clear information about what needs to be done and by when Ensure the scheduler has a voice on the project during implementation Support the scheduler in communicating to users Ensure the scheduler knows where to find help	Ensure the schedulers contribution is acknowledged Acknowledge impact Seek and listen to feedback
Those who will use the new product or service Level of comfort with ambiguity: low	Experience the change/ solution	Create early awareness Make information available	Make sure information is available	Raise awareness Signpost indicative timescales Ensure the users understands what the project means for me Seek and listen to feedback Check readiness	Provide clear advice on what the user needs to do and when Seek and listen to feedback	Ensure the users contribution is acknowledged. Acknowledge impact Seek and listen to feedback

be supportive if he or she does not understand the benefits or does not have confidence in the project team to deliver. Without clear objectives for the relationship it will be unfocussed, risking wasting the time of the stakeholder and the relationship owner.

Moving stakeholders through awareness and understanding towards support and commitment to the project calls for a mix of approaches. Initially, there will be a need to inform and explain the project. Outline the rationale or case for change and the benefits. Share the vision, or involve the stakeholder in its development. Explain the timescales, the approach to delivery and governance arrangements. From here, with the stakeholder now well informed, a two-way dialogue can be developed giving stakeholders the opportunity to input their ideas.

It is this opportunity for involvement at an early stage that is most likely to result in support, but the information stage is important too; the stakeholder needs to understand the project before he or she can contribute usefully.

Throughout this process, the role of the project communicator is to provide content and tools that can help to facilitate these conversations. This can take a number of forms, for example:

- Briefing pack: this can include answers to frequently asked questions, a biography of the stakeholder, a summary of previous contact with the stakeholder, a note of their key concerns and areas of interest, plus meeting feedback template (see the Project Communicator's Toolkit example at the end of the chapter).

- Core presentation pack that can be used to support group discussions.

- Project key facts document – the key points summarised.

- Brochure or leaflet about the project.

MATCHING THE APPROACH TO THE TRADITIONAL POWER/ INTEREST ANALYSIS

Stakeholder analysis: key players

The approach here should be to assign relationship owners and make face-to-face the priority. This approach has a number of advantages:

- the stakeholder has a single point of contact;

- the stakeholder feels that he or she is valued;

- the risk of conflicting messages or duplication of activity is reduced;

- feedback can be gathered quickly.

This ownership of a stakeholder needs to be planned and measured. The communication role here is to work with the owner to build an engagement plan. This should include:

- how regularly meetings will be held;

- the format of these meetings;

- supporting materials and messages to be provided;

- what other communication methods will be used;

- how the relationship will be evaluated.

It is essential that there is a feedback loop and the views of the stakeholder fed back into the programme in a structured way. The communication function can collate the feedback and look for trends. It may be helpful to use a feedback template to ensure that there is some structure. This could capture:

- date of meeting;

- messages communicated;

- summary of stakeholder's views;

- suggested next steps.

Getting the relationship right is important. While the project communicator may own the relationship with some stakeholders (for example other communicators), it is members of the project team and project sponsors that will own the majority of the relationships. Even though a sponsor has themselves been identified as a stakeholder, it may be appropriate to call on him or her to help implement the stakeholder engagement strategy. Think about the grade or level of the relationship owner in relation to the stakeholder; consider whether the stakeholder would expect to hear from a peer for example.

Stakeholder analysis: keep satisfied

Members of this group should also be assigned a relationship owner. Face-to-face engagement can be combined with other channels.

Those in this category are there because they have power or influence. Their interest in the project isn't high and – unless the project needs them to be proactive on its behalf – it is probably acceptable for them to stay this way and this means ensuring that they are kept satisfied.

An element of face-to-face contact is appropriate and can be planned as for key players, but probably does not need to be as intense.

Other forms of communication should be considered to supplement face-to-face contact. As these are likely to be busy people, email updates and newsletters probably aren't ideal. Try to find smarter ways to get project messages to them, consider:

- giving updates to any boards or groups that they attend;

- find out what communication channels exist and are already working for the stakeholder and see if project messages can be included;

- joining up with messages from other programmes and projects.

Stakeholder analysis: inform

Stakeholders who fall into this category can be kept up to date through a range of means such as:

- regular emails – but not too many, remember they don't have a lot of interest;

- via existing channels (organisation magazine and so on);

- joining up with messages from other programmes and projects.

Stakeholder analysis: consult

This group is interested but has been judged to be of low influence. As already discussed at the analysis stage, this group's lack of influence is not necessarily a reason to give them a low priority – depending on the project and which stakeholders have been put into this category, it could be considered unethical not to involve them.

True consultation means listening to a group of stakeholders and being prepared to act on their feedback where possible. The term is used a lot in the public sector but doesn't always equate to true two-way dialogue. The approach will need to be supported with sufficient information for the stakeholders to make a meaningful contribution.

Decisions about the approach to the stakeholder relationship can be included in the communication and stakeholder engagement strategy.

Step 4: Plan

Having decided on the right approach to engaging with each stakeholder, the next step is to plan the engagement activity.

The aim with the plan is to:

- Ensure that key stakeholders aren't being forgotten: the plan should provide a visual overview of stakeholder contact making it easy to see which stakeholders may not have been contacted for some time. Remember to also capture on the plan contact that happens through the governance process, for example attendance at board meetings. The aim is to have a complete picture of that stakeholder's relationship with the project.

- Help to ensure that stakeholders don't receive multiple contacts from the project: this happens too often on projects, somebody from the team arrives to meet with a stakeholder to find that a colleague has just met with them. It wastes the stakeholder's time and makes the project look unco-ordinated and badly managed. To avoid this happening it is necessary to make the project team aware of the stakeholder plan and require them to check before they contact a stakeholder and report back afterwards. This can seem onerous, so try and find a way to make it as simple as possible for everyone to follow the process. Reviewing and reporting on stakeholder activity at checkpoint meetings when key project team members are all together can be a useful way to do this.

- Spot trends and issues early on: having a central view of stakeholder concerns will enable the project communicator to spot trends and emerging issues. Steps can then be taken in conjunction with relationship owners to address them quickly.

- Ensure that project messages are consistent in terms of content and timing: stakeholders need to receive consistent messages about the project at more or less the same time. Of course unless every stakeholder is to be met on the same day, this isn't always practical. The importance of this principle depends on the importance of the message. A general project update isn't so critical in terms of timing, but if something fundamental has changed then it is important to ensure that key stakeholders aren't left uninformed. There is a distinction to be made between routine stakeholder meetings and important announcements. A key project announcement should be the subject of a specific communication plan which ensures that everyone who needs to know hears at the right time and in the right order.

Depending on the stage of the project, this stakeholder plan can be captured separately to the communication plan and be ordered by stakeholder rather than by date (which is how a communication plan is usually presented). This document is sometimes known as a 'stakeholder tracker' (because it tracks contact with stakeholders). There is more about planning in Chapter 6.

Step 5: Review and Update

Evaluate stakeholder relationships in a structured way. The stakeholder engagement plan should be reviewed regularly with the project leadership team. As well as discussing the stakeholders' views, check whether the process is working for everyone and whether the relationship owners are right. If a stakeholder is expressing concerns, do they need to be seen more regularly for example?

From time to time there can be value in adopting a more scientific approach to evaluating stakeholder relationships. The views of the relationship owner are important but they are subjective and difficult to compare with those of other relationship owners. Conducting a more scientifically based piece of research will provide more robust data.

Key stakeholders are likely to be busy and often senior people; they may not always be open to being surveyed, however some may be pleased that the project is taking the time to find out their views in a structured way.

A simple telephone survey 'pulse check' conducted by the project communicator may suffice. Design the research with care; keep it short with questions that are easy to answer. There is an example in the Project Communicator's Toolkit at the end of the chapter.

Keep the status of stakeholders under review and revise the plan if you need to.

Diary a review of the stakeholder analysis to happen, say, quarterly. This should be a short workshop where relationship owners are involved. The output should be a revised stakeholder map reflecting any changes in stakeholders and their priority.

Working with Unions and Staff Groups

Ownership of the trade union relationship does not always rest with project communications. There may well be an HR or employee relations representative charged with engaging with this group. The role for communications is to ensure that messages and activity are aligned with that for other stakeholders.

This can take careful planning, but is usually just a case of getting things in the right order. Unions or staff groups may expect to see communication materials in advance of them going to staff – although this may depend on the extent of the changes being planned. They will of course be most interested when the project is changing, removing or creating jobs.

Clearly it doesn't pay to get this relationship wrong, so seek advice from employee relations experts in the organisation and ensure that this important stakeholder group and their expectations are built into communication planning.

Unions and staff groups can provide valuable insights into the mood of the organisation and will also be sighted on other change projects so may spot synergies or potential clashes.

Stakeholders within the Project

Internal project communication should follow the same principles. Colleagues will have different requirements in terms of what they need to know.

Project board and checkpoint meetings should always have communication on the agenda. However, this is often the last on the list and the item that gets cut when the meeting over runs. So, it can be more effective for the project communicator to prompt a discussion about communication for each decision that is made at the meeting. Sometimes, simply asking the questions: 'Who needs to know?' and 'Who is going to tell them?' is all that is needed. Asking who is going to do the telling is important because it will not always be appropriate for this to be the role of the project communicator. Work stream leaders at the meeting should take responsibility for informing their teams. The role of the communication function here is to prompt the discussion, help clarify the message and ensure that the action is captured. Of course key decisions and discussions may need to be communicated widely in which case the project communicator is likely to be best placed to make sure that this happens.

Summary

This chapter sets out a planned approach to working with stakeholders. Communicators have an important role to play in developing stakeholder relationships and should take ownership of the process or be at the heart if that ownership should sit elsewhere. Models for analysing stakeholders have been given including one designed specifically for a project setting and which includes what is required of the stakeholder and the communicator's role.

Project Communicator's Toolkit: Example Stakeholder Feedback Summary

Relationship owners should be encouraged to capture feedback from stakeholder meetings in a structured way. A simple template can be provided to help them to do this. The information is then transferred to the stakeholder plan or tracker. As always, think about how things are written, if the stakeholder would not like to read it, don't write it.

Stakeholder	Mary Jones, Director of HR
Relationship owner	Susan Smith, project manager
Date of meeting	16 February
Key themes discussed	
Concerns expressed	
Stakeholder's perception of project	
Next steps agreed	

Project Communicator's Toolkit: Pulse Survey for Capturing Stakeholder Feedback

Stakeholder views can be captured through a quick 'pulse' survey. The questions asked should relate back to the objectives set for the relationship and should cover both outputs and outcomes:

- Outputs – is the level of contact about right, are messages clear and helpful?

- Outcomes – for example, about understanding of the project, support, trust in the project team, and confidence in the ability to deliver.

A short survey of about five questions is probably right and usually no more than 10. A scale of strongly agree to strongly disagree (known as a Likert scale) can be a quick and effective way to gauge opinion. The type of questions asked will depend on the objectives set for the relationship but some example questions are as follows, using a scale of 'Strongly agree, agree, neither agree or disagree, disagree, strongly disagree':

- The amount of contact of that I have with the project is about right.

- I know who to go to if I have questions or concerns.

- I feel I can trust the project leadership.

- My views about the project are listened to.

- I have confidence in the project team to deliver.

For more about research and evaluation, see Chapter 7.

4

Creating Great Content

Having completed the strategic planning phase, attention can be turned to creating communication content. This is often seen as the more fun part of the communication role, but it is important to wait until the strategic planning stages are complete because only then can the content be designed to help deliver the objectives in the strategy and be appropriate to the stakeholder. Making the mistake of jumping into creating content without an understanding of what needs to be achieved or who the content is aimed at is unlikely to produce the desired outcomes.

Communication content can be written, visual and verbal. Generating content is an area of communication where good technical communication skills are needed. Drafting written copy that is well structured and engaging in style comes with training and practice. It calls for a different type of written style to report writing or the style of an essay written at university. If the skills don't exist within the project communication team it is a skill that may be worth buying in. Busy stakeholders will be grateful for a communication that gets to the point and doesn't need to be read more than once to get the gist. Visual content too should look professional, it may be the first experience that a stakeholder has of a project and first impressions count. Professional doesn't mean glossy and expensive – in fact that may do more harm than good especially if the project is aiming to realise financial benefits. In terms of video, the growth of social media has enabled individuals to record and share content on personal devices. As a result audiences are much more accepting of content that is less 'produced' and which often has a more authentic feel. Verbal communication needs to be thought about just as carefully. Just because someone is a good project manager or senior sponsor doesn't mean that they will be comfortable standing up in front of the team or stakeholders. There may be a need for coaching not only in the messages to be delivered but in the style of delivery too.

This chapter is designed to help the project communicator develop great content that is engaging and right for the stakeholder, it covers:

- tone of voice including branding;

- story telling;

- joining up messages;

- stakeholder-centred communication;

- written communication: hints and tips.

Tone of Voice

Tone of voice is as much about how something is said as what is said. Successful brands have a consistent tone of voice and projects are no different. Tone of voice isn't only about using Plain English – which is essential for any project – but it is also about the personality that comes through in the communication. The tone of voice becomes part of the message – the way something is said has as much impact as the message that is being communicated. Is the tone of voice for the project friendly and chatty or serious and official?

Getting the tone of voice right for the project matters because:

- It demonstrates the project's attitude to its stakeholders – for example, content that is full of project jargon suggests that nobody on the project has thought or cares whether it will make sense to anyone else.

- It brings with it consistency in language across all communication which helps with understanding.

- A consistent tone of voice looks professional, helping to win the respect of stakeholders.

Where the project is part of a wider organisation, it needs to consider whether its tone of voice should match that of the organisation. Generally speaking the answer to this question is that yes it should. However, there may be a case for the project adopting a different tone of voice if it is bringing about change or the wider organisation does not have a defined tone of voice (which is sometimes the case). So if the project is designed, for example, to bring about modernisation or improve customer service, adopting a friendlier more informal style than the wider organisation usually uses may be appropriate. However care needs to be taken not to alienate stakeholders by being so 'out there' that they disengage.

THE TROUBLE WITH JARGON

Typical project jargon includes acronyms, technical language and 'business speak'. It is inconsistent with a Plain English approach to communication.

Jargon can be useful shorthand for project colleagues, long complicated names and descriptions can be reduced to a handy 'TLA' (three letter acronyms). The problem is that not everyone in the project will know what is meant and their use can spill over into communication beyond the project team leaving stakeholders baffled and alienated. A glossary of terms can be useful, but this isn't any substitute for using Plain English so take care not to solve the problem of impenetrable language with a glossary; far better to address the root cause and avoid jargon in the first place.

Some language will be understood easily by project colleagues (for example the name of an IT system such as ERP which stands for Enterprise Resource Planning) but is unlikely to be understood by many stakeholders so should be avoided. Never assume that everyone on the project understands either. People may be reluctant to speak up for fear of looking silly, so the role of communication should be to champion Plain English within the project and to speak up when communication isn't clear.

WHAT'S IN A NAME?

One of the early decisions in the project lifecycle is what to call it. This can be one of the first communication opportunities and is important to get right – it sets the tone of things to come. Think carefully before embarking on a naming competition. This is often a misguided attempt to engage people in the change. The chances are the result will be a selection of contrived acronyms, Greek myths and metrological phenomenon. This trend for names that bear no relation to the work in hand is fair enough if the output of the project is competitively sensitive – for example a new product is in development, but many projects want the complete opposite – awareness and engagement.

By selecting a name that explains what the project is doing, the message being sent is that the project is open and accessible. A name that has to be explained before it can be understood sets up barriers instantly. Stakeholders have to be 'in the know' or waste time trying to find out what it's all about.

However, coming up with such a name can be easier said than done – finding a form of words that encapsulates the project yet is short and easy to say is difficult. The danger is that whatever name is given, people will try and reduce it to an acronym. It is worth spending some time to get it right and perhaps test it with a few people outside the project.

BRAND IDENTITY

Think of any well known and respected brand; it will, without a doubt, be consistent in the way that it presents itself. There will be coherence in its imagery and tone of voice, whether internal or external. It does this because a strong brand identity aids buying decisions and represents a set of brand values. Brand identity covers things like the colours, fonts and images but also language and values.

The project is going to produce documentation and probably communication materials (brochures, web pages and so on) and there are similar, strong advantages to creating a consistent look and feel:

- easy recognition of the project by stakeholders;

- alignment with a wider corporate identity (or perhaps programme or portfolio identity);

- professional look and feel.

It can be tempting to create a separate identity for the project, but be cautious here. There are many advantages, but also pitfalls in creating a specific identity:

- The project can look transient – yet another initiative with a wacky name and logo that is here today and gone tomorrow. Drawing on the corporate identity of the organisation of which the project is a part sends the message that the project is a core part of the overarching organisational strategy and there is commitment to it at senior level.

- It creates a confusing picture for stakeholders who can be left wondering how the project fits with everything else that is happening in an organisation.

- Potential clashes with the organisation's central communication function and brand team whose role it is to protect the brand and corporate identity.

- Cost. Who is going to do the design work? It is expensive and time consuming to come up with a brand identity from scratch (if it is to be done well, which of course it should be).

Should it be decided to adopt a brand identity specifically for the project, then it must be protected in the same way that any popular consumer brand would protect theirs. Again, remember that design is a job for the professionals. There is a template design brief as part of the Project Communicator's Toolkit at the end of this chapter. Having said that, it isn't always desirable or possible to spend a lot of money on design work, so invest some time upfront in creating a suite of materials that is flexible and can be adapted within the project while maintaining design integrity.

If the project is going to adopt the brand identity of the organisation of which it is a part then there will probably be a set of brand guidelines in existence. These will set out how the logo should and should not be used plus the fonts, colours and maybe even photography or other images that support it.

Whatever approach is taken, once adopted, brand guidelines should be adhered to. Avoid the temptation to adapt, tweak or stretch the logo, it will only end up looking messy and amateur.

Story Telling

Story telling comes naturally. It is part of every culture with stories being told through books, theatre, film and music and of course every day people are telling each other stories about things that have happened to them. Everyone loves a good story. They are easy to remember – most people can still explain the essence of a movie that they have seen some time after having seen it and usually do so in no more than a few sentences. Stories are told and retold within organisations too; people use them to make sense of what is happening now by talking about what has happened in the past. These stories contribute to the development of a corporate culture and listening to the stories that are told is one way of beginning to understand the culture of an organisation. Of course, these stories are created and shared informally without the purposeful involvement of the organisation itself, but story telling can also be used to good effect by a project to explain what is happening. Some people may find the term 'story' off putting; they may feel that it doesn't sound serious enough for the task in hand. The word 'narrative' can be used instead, although this does sound rather like 'corporate speak' but if it helps project colleagues and sponsors buy in to the idea of story telling then it is worth using. Listen how politicians will often use stories to make a policy point much more interesting: 'I met a lady in Birmingham who had been waiting for a knee operation for six months' is much more powerful than a simply factual statement that says, 'Hospital waiting lists are too long'.

Story telling can be used in a number of ways in projects for example to explain:

- the rationale for a change project;

- how a project fits in with wider corporate objectives;

- how a new product, system or way of working was arrived at;

- how things will feel once the project is complete, perhaps through a 'day in the life' story.

WHAT MAKES A GOOD STORY?

There are many books specifically on the topic of corporate story telling, but one quick and easy way to understand what makes a compelling and memorable story is to look no further than the media. Look out for stories that are told and retold across different media, stories that friends and colleagues are discussing and then analyse what makes them so interesting. There are some common themes:

- something unexpected;

- something incongruous;

- human interest;

- something that people can relate to 'that could be me'.

A good example of something incongruous was the story about the body of King Richard III found under a car park. This was a major news story in the UK during 2013. The body of the last Plantagenet king was discovered under a car park in the city of Leicester. The fact that the discovery was made under a car park was the main thrust of almost every news story and is probably the thing that most people remember. It works as a story because it 'paints' a picture and because of the contrast and incongruity of the situation – royalty and car parks don't normally go together. Had the discovery been made under some romantic abbey ruins in a leafy cathedral city in southern England would the story have had the same impact or been told in the same way? Probably not.

Another good example is the UK Prime Minister's new baby daughter sleeping in a cardboard box. When a new daughter of Prime Minister David Cameron and his wife Samantha was born prematurely while the couple were on holiday in the Cornwall in the south west of England, she spent the first few nights of her life sleeping in a cardboard box decorated by her older sister because – not expecting her arrival – the couple did not have a cot for her. The story was widely reported and again is memorable because one would not expect the Prime Minister's child to sleep in a box!

Of course people will read this story differently according to factors such as their political views. Some may think it a lovely story that paints a picture of happy family life. Others may see it more cynically as a story placed with the media to make the couple seem more human. Stories will be interpreted according to the stakeholder's experiences and views of the world. What may seem a charming and innocent story to one person can look calculating and like propaganda to another. There is more about the theory of communication and how we interpret messages in the Vignette at the end of this chapter.

TELLING A STORY ABOUT THE PROJECT VISION

Communication of the vision should be ongoing because it provides the context and rationale for all project activity. Communicating the vision doesn't mean simply displaying it on posters or on leaflets. While these tactics have their place the vision should form part of the story – or narrative – that is told about the project, its milestones and achievements.

This is an important function of leadership communication with the project team. The project manager and senior sponsors should fit things like achievements and new tasks in to the context of the vision. This should be done across all channels, for example verbally in team meetings and in written communication including project documentation.

If working in a programme or portfolio environment, then this approach should flow throughout. Communicating the vision by telling a story is not only effective, but it enables people to put things into their own words while still staying true to the vision. There is more about vision statements in the Vignette at the end of this chapter.

Joining It All Up

Joining up project messages with other messages going to the same stakeholders makes good sense. It shows people how everything fits together, rather than leaving them to try and work it out for themselves (they probably won't bother). It can also reduce the amount of communication that people receive, meaning that messages are more likely to be heard.

If the project is part of a programme and maybe a portfolio, then this is the first place to look for content for that joined-up story. Links can also be made to the wider organisation and the external environment – it is here where the rationale for the project can be found, see Figure 4.1. The rationale from the project comes from the top down and the project story must also support the organisation, portfolio and programme strategies.

Piggy-backing on other messages is also a good way of raising awareness in the early stages of a project when there isn't much to say. It may not be appropriate to go out with standalone messages when delivery is a long way off, but incorporating awareness messages in other communications that are happening is an effective and controlled way of starting to tell the project story. Any project will be part of a wider strategy or vision, so whenever that bigger picture is being discussed, ensure that project messages are being included as appropriate. This means working closely with other communicators at the corporate level or on other projects to ensure that this can happen. For example if a company CEO is talking to staff about the vision or plans for the year ahead, any project that is contributing to this can be mentioned at the same time helping to demonstrate how everything fits together and creating awareness of the project in context.

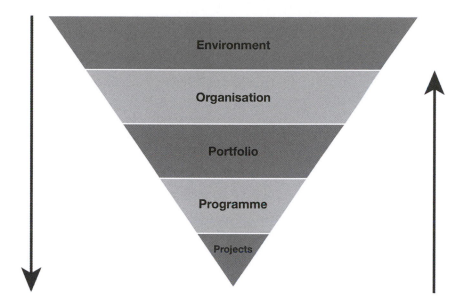

Figure 4.1   Telling a joined-up story, the flow of messages

Leadership Communication

Effective leadership communication can make a big difference to the success of the project communication effort. To do this it needs to be credible, authentic and 'on message', suggestions to help achieve this follow.

CREDIBILITY

Project leaders need to be credible communicators. Credibility comes from a number of factors. Perloff (2008) identified:

- Expertise: the communicator is seen as having special skills or know-how.

- Trustworthiness: the communicator is perceived as honest and of good character.

- Goodwill: the communicator who displays goodwill shows that he or she has the listeners' interests at heart, understands the views of others and is empathic towards the problems that the audience may be experiencing.

The project communicator can help to draw out these characteristics in project leaders. Ways that this might achieved can include:

- feature articles talking about the person's background, previous projects and so on;

- ensuring that all communication is open and honest;

- ensuring that the concerns of stakeholders are heard and acknowledged.

AUTHENTICITY

Leaders also need to be seen as authentic. It can seem counter-intuitive to talk about managing communication in order to achieve authenticity, but this style of communication can seem alien to project leaders who have been accustomed to very formal methods of communication and feel compelled to say everything is fine when it isn't. They may need coaching and support in being themselves when they communicate. This is particularly important when using social media as a form of project communication. This is a medium that is all about authenticity and content that is clearly corporate and highly managed will undermine trust and confidence. Readers can always tell when a blog post has been written by the communication team, not the project manager!

Of course not every leader is a Steve Jobs or a Richard Branson and the key is for them to find their own style and feel comfortable in their role as a communicator. The style still needs to be appropriate for the audience, the message and the channel. Announcing that the project is in difficulties will demand a different tone to announcing that a major milestone has been achieved.

There may be hurdles to overcome in helping leaders to achieve a more authentic communication style, but this is where project communication can add real value by providing coaching and support. Some of the blockers to an authentic communication style are outlined in Table 4.1.

Table 4.1   Overcoming blockers to authentic leadership communication

Blocker to authentic communication, project leaders may:	Project communicators can help by:
Feel that long words and lots of corporate management language is what is expected of them.	Gathering feedback on communication to share with the leader, showing where language that is too corporate is alienating stakeholders.
See it as 'dumbing down'.	Try sharing authoritative writing that is written simply with project leaders to show how effective it can be. Even broadsheet newspapers are written so that they can be understood by a seven year old child. Achieving simplicity in language is highly skilled.
Be concerned that being too open will encourage questions to which they don't know they answer.	Remind project leaders that they do not have to know the answer to everything. Equip them with handling strategies when questions arise. This may be as simple as promising to find out and respond or explaining why the answer isn't known and when it will be. Being honest about not knowing will win the respect of stakeholders.
Worry about saying something commercially sensitive or inappropriate.	People respect honesty, if some information can't be given because it is commercially sensitive, simply say so, but take care that this doesn't look like an excuse for not sharing information. Equip leaders with possible responses to questions that fall into this category so that at least some information can be given.
Believe that saying everything is fine when it isn't, is motivational.	Everyone on the project will know what the real position is. The project leadership needs to acknowledge any problems and set out how they are to be addressed. People will respect this honesty. Anything else will feel like 'spin' and can seem insulting to colleagues who feel that they can't be trusted with the truth.

ON MESSAGE

Even the most natural communicator can need support from the communication function in ensuring that the right messages are being delivered and in a way that is right for the audience. Taking every opportunity to remind project leaders of the key messages will help to avoid confusion in the project and with stakeholders. Confirm and agree key messages:

- before any stakeholder meetings, presentations and so on;

- at the end of meetings such as checkpoints and project boards to ensure everyone goes away with a consistent understanding of what has or hasn't been decided. In addition to agreeing the messages, be clear about to whom and by whom they will be communicated. This is essential otherwise some will leave the meeting unsure about what they can say so say nothing, while others will head back to their desk and tell their teams everything.

Stakeholder-centred Communication

The stakeholder needs to come first when preparing communication content. This sounds obvious, but it can be easy for projects to forget this and think about what it wants to tell people, rather than what people want to know.

In the following example the programme leadership goes into a communication event with a clear idea of what it wants to say, but no thought given to the audience.

> *Two companies were merging and a new director had been brought in to head up the new organisation. Managers across both organisations knew that the merger would result in less management jobs being available.*

> *The merger programme set up a series of briefings where the new director spoke to managers. He opened the meetings by saying that he was not going to discuss jobs but wanted to focus on the vision for the new organisation. He wanted to motivate the managers and ensure that they understood the vision. However, the managers felt that he didn't have any empathy and didn't care about what mattered to them. As a result they came away disillusioned and couldn't even recall what had been said about the vision.*

What the director should have done was acknowledge the job issue at the start and set out a timeline for when decisions about jobs would be made together with the process and how they could help to shape the outcome. It is arguable whether this was the right forum to discuss the vision at all, given that most of the audience were more concerned about their jobs. The programme and leadership team missed the fact that this important group of stakeholders was at a different point in the change curve (see Chapter 2, Figure 2.3). The leadership team – who were all confirmed in their roles – were clearly several steps ahead in terms of being ready for the change but had failed to acknowledge the need to support others who were some steps behind.

The lessons from this example are that before crafting a communication ask:

* Who is this message for?

* What will they be concerned about?

- How do they like to receive communications?

- What might be their preferred communication style? For example, highly detailed or quick and easy to digest?

- What else is happening to these people that might influence the message?

- Are there any cultural considerations?

If in doubt, the thing to do is ask people; involve some stakeholders in reviewing and signing off content. Testing something before issuing it is time well spent and also a good opportunity to get stakeholders involved. People will be happy to help and pleased that someone took the time to ask them what they thought.

Written Communication: Hints and Tips

Making written communication clear and engaging is a skill, making it unambiguous is almost impossible! The way that somebody interprets the message will always be influenced by their own personal view and circumstances. However, there are some principles that project communicators can follow that will help to ensure that messages are clear and as easy as possible to understand.

KIS: KEEP IT SIMPLE

Often in the workplace, people can slip into a form of writing that is overly wordy and full of jargon because they think that this is what is expected. Project communicators need to challenge this.

Simple, clear writing is highly skilled. Whatever one may think about the tabloid press, to be able to condense a complicated story into a couple of paragraphs takes skill. But it isn't just the tabloids that keep things simple, all media write their stories in a way that is easy to understand. Journalists are taught to write their stories as though writing for a seven year old – even on a traditional broadsheet newspaper.

This is an important point, because it proves that clear writing is not necessarily associated with dumbing down a message.

WHAT IS THE DESIRED OUTCOME OF THE COMMUNICATION?

There needs to be a clear objective for the communication that is relevant to the audience that will receive it. What is the desired outcome? If this can't be identified then there may not be a need for the communication at all. It isn't sufficient for a member of the project team to want to tell people something, there has to be a good reason, otherwise it isn't an audience-centred piece of communication.

GET THE STRUCTURE RIGHT

Once the objective is clear, think about the structure. Put the point of the message at the start. Tell people if it contains something that they need to do or if it is just for information. This will be appreciated because it helps people to manage the flow of communications that they will be receiving from a number of sources – they can prioritise more easily.

Think of a written communication like an upside down pyramid (see Figure 4.2) with the most important message right at the top with the importance of the content reducing the further down you go. Once written, a useful test is to cover up everything but the first paragraph and see if it contains the key point. Try this test on a story in a newspaper to see how it works. Essentially the test is to make sure that if someone reads no further than the first paragraph, they will still have read the most important message.

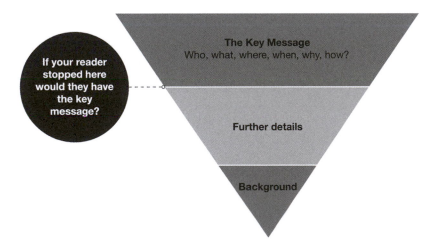

Figure 4.2   **Good written communication gets straight to the point**

WHAT DOES IT MEAN TO ME?

Check that the communication explains what it means for the reader. Often people talk in terms of 'what's in it for me?' but this implies that the reader must be 'sold' the message which may not always be appropriate and is a very one-way approach to communication. There won't always be a positive outcome for everyone and projects need to be honest about this. So instead think in terms of *what it means to* individuals; for example how will it affect their jobs?

Creating a House Style

A house style sets out how things will be written. They are used extensively in the media but also have a place within organisations and of course projects. Having a house style means that there is a consistent way of using language. Just as brand guidelines set out how an organisation's logo can and can't be used together with what colours and fonts should be employed, a house style does the same for language. It can also be extended to address some of the common grammatical errors that can be made.

Consistency in language is important because it:

- looks more professional;

- helps to avoid misunderstandings;

- helps ensure accuracy;

- helps avoid use of terms that are considered unacceptable in the particular workplace (for example, perhaps because they are outdated or there are cultural sensitivities in different countries);

- can link the project to the wider organisation.

The first step when introducing a project house style is to check whether the wider organisation of which the project is part has one in place (or whether there is one at programme level). If it does, this should of course be followed and project-specific information added to it. There are so many variations on what could be included depending on the project that it isn't possible to list them all, but as a guide project-specific content may include:

- How to refer to the project, for example can the name be abbreviated?

- Names of any systems or services that are part of the project and how to refer to them.

- How does the project refer to those with which it is working? For example, as suppliers or partners?

If no house style is in place it is a good idea to create one for the project. A typical, generic internal house style will include guidance on:

- use of upper case letters (for example are they used on job titles?);

- how numbers are written;

- how dates are written;

- how the project is referred to;

- when and what abbreviations are acceptable;

- grammatical guidance and style of punctuation.

The house style can be owned and maintained by the communication function or by the project management office (PMO). Wherever ownership rests, project communication should be involved to ensure that it promotes consistency and Plain English communication.

An example house style document is given at the end of this chapter as part of the Project Communicator's Toolkit.

Sign-off Protocols

The final step in creating great content is to get it approved. Communication messages and materials will need to be approved by someone senior within the project team or maybe by sponsors.

Agreeing how this will happen and setting this out in a set of sign-off protocols at the start of the project can save time because everyone will know what their responsibility is and the timescales to which they must work.

Getting formal sign-off can be onerous, but it is important to do for the following reasons:

- it helps to ensure accuracy;

- it may highlight misunderstandings within the project;

- it helps to get buy-in to the communication activity;

- it raises the profile of the communication function and provides a good opportunity for the communication function to enter into a dialogue with the project leadership.

Achieving signoff can be one of the most frustrating aspects of the project communicator's job, sometimes by the time something is signed off the situation has changed and the communication is out of date. This is because projects move at a fast pace and, particularly in the initiation, design and test stages, things are changing all the time. For this reason the sign-off of project communications has to be as quick and flexible as possible.

This is another reason why project communication needs to be represented at the top of the project – the greater the understanding that the communicator has, the more likely it is that communication is going to be accurate, fit for purpose and signed off quickly with minimum changes.

The sign-off protocol can sit as part of the communication strategy, or be a document in its own right. It can be extended to cover who should input into the formation of communication messages. There is an example in the Project Communicator's Toolkit at the end of this chapter.

Summary

This chapter has looked at how to produce great content for project communication. However, even the best crafted content can't produce the best outcome if it isn't delivering a well thought through strategy. Often the communication function is expected to jump straight into 'delivery mode' but this is a mistake because how will the communicator know what to say and to whom? The best outcomes result from content that is audience-centred and delivered in a clear and engaging way.

Project Communicator's Toolkit: Example House Style Guide

The following template provides a useful starting point for the project or programme communicator wanting to create a house style. It provides guidance on things like grammar, Plain English and words that can cause confusion (see Table 4.2). Items in italics show where the guide can be adapted to the project or programme.

Table 4.2   Words that can cause confusion

Words that can cause confusion	
Government	Usually with a lower case 'g', unless at the start of a sentence of course. Or where referring to a specific government, for example the French Government.
Parliament	Usually upper case, unless talking about a country. For example 'the French parliament'.
Internet and intranet	Neither need a capital 'I' (unless at the start of a sentence).
Online	Use a lower case 'o' and make it one word.
Home page	Is two words.
Include any other terms that might be specific to the project/programme or the organisation.	

ABOUT THIS GUIDE

This guide is for people working on the (name) project/programme. It is designed to help us write in a clear and consistent way. It should be read in conjunction with the organisation's house style (where this exists, include link or location).

Having a clear and consistent style makes things easier to read, makes us look professional.

PLAIN ENGLISH – SOME TIPS

- Before you decide what to write, ask yourself who your audience is and what they want to know. You need to be clear about who you are talking to before you decide what information to include and what tone to use.

- Always use language that everyone can understand. Plain English is good English, not 'dumbed down' English.

- Use common, everyday words and avoid technical jargon or formal words.

- Use short sentences (ideally 15 to 20 words).

- Avoid using too many acronyms and abbreviations. If you need to use one, always give the name in full at first, followed by the acronym or abbreviation in brackets. After that, you can use the acronym or abbreviation only. Let's try not to create any new ones.

- Use active rather than passive verbs, essentially this means attaching the verb to whoever is doing something. For example:

    - Active: the company launched the system.
    - Passive: the system was launched.

- Try to use 'we' and 'you' where appropriate. It makes the tone much friendlier and it also helps to make the meaning of your text clearer.

- If possible, get a colleague to read your text through before you publish it. If your colleague cannot understand what it means, try to rewrite it until they can.

ABBREVIATIONS AND ACRONYMS

Although in general you should avoid abbreviations and acronyms, if an organisation's name or a particular term appears frequently, you should refer to it in full the first time followed by its initials in brackets, and from then on by just the letters. Everyday abbreviations (such as BBC, DNA and IT) and acronyms such as laser and radar do not need their full names. (*Specific instructions about any acronyms or abbreviations in common use on the project or programme can be added here.*)

BULLET POINTS

There are two ways to write bullet points.

If the introduction to the list is a complete sentence, each bullet point should also be a complete sentence. You do not need to use semi-colons to separate them. Each bullet begins with a capital letter and ends with a full stop. An example is given below.

Everyone on the project must observe the house style because it helps good communication.

- You need to check when it is and isn't appropriate to use capital letters.

- The house style provides a useful guide to words specific to the organisation.

- Following the house style make the project look professional.

If the opening sentence does not end with a full stop (or question mark) then each bullet point starts with a lower case letter and be separated by a semi colon. An example is given below.

Working closely with your communication team is important because:

- they understand the best way to communicate with stakeholders;

- it can help you to ensure that the project reaches its milestones;

- you can concentrate on your role, while the professional communicators manager communication activity.

CAPITAL LETTERS

Use capital letters sparingly and only when appropriate. Never use them for emphasis; they are actually harder to read than normal type.

- Job titles: generic job titles usually start with a lower case letter. For example, 'manager', 'customer service assistant'.

- Companies and organisations: these are names, so should have an upper case letter.

DATES

For specific dates, write the day first in figures (without 'st', 'nd', 'rd' or 'th') followed by the month and the year in full. Do not separate the parts of the date by commas (for example, write '1 January 2008').

For general dates, you need to include 'st', 'nd', 'rd' or 'th' to make the meaning clear. For example, 'Team meetings are held on the 12th of the month.'

TYPE SIZE AND LEGIBILITY

Use the simple, clear typeface Arial (or other font as directed by the programme or organisation).

Use a minimum text size of 11 point, although 14 point is recommended if you want to be accessible to more people. Estimates show that 75 per cent of visually impaired people can read 14 point text.

For PowerPoint, Arial or Verdana is recommended and no text should ever be smaller than 18 point when used for presentations. As a general rule, if you have to tell your audience 'you won't be able to read this but...' don't use the slide!

CULTURAL TERMS

Any culturally specific terms and guidance should be included here.

GLOSSARY

A glossary can be a useful addition to your house style, it can:

- define key terms;

- clarify words and terms which should and shouldn't be used (for example a role title that may have been reviewed and updated);

- explain acronyms and abbreviations (although remember that these should be kept to a minimum).

Project Communicator's Toolkit: Sign-off Protocol

As part of the communication strategy it can be helpful to set out how communication materials will be signed off. This ensures that everyone knows the process and what is expected of them. An example sign-off protocol is given below at Table 4.3.

Table 4.3   Project Communicator's Toolkit: sign-off protocol

Type of communication	Input required from	Reviewed by	Timescale	Final approval	Timescale
Weekly newsletter*	Work stream leads Project manager	Content providers review their items	Two working days	Project manager	Two working days

*For a weekly communication, consider adding the day and possibly time that sign-off will be required and put it into the appropriate peoples' diaries.

Project Communicator's Toolkit: Briefing a Designer

The design process should be a collaborative and enjoyable one but to achieve this, the designer needs a good brief to work from. It helps to avoid misunderstandings and keeps costs down by minimising rework. The following is a suggested structure for a design brief.

- Background: explain in a couple of paragraphs what the project is doing and why. Include how it fits into the organisation's strategy and whether it is part of a programme. If it is, explain the aim of the programme.

- Target audience: explain who the design concept or collateral will be seen by. Give as much information about them as possible.

- How the design or materials will be used and distributed: do print materials need a long shelf life? Will they be posted or handed out?

- Timescales: provide details of what will be needed and by when. Remember to build in contingency time. Ensure that the timescales reflect the timings in the communication plan and project plan, which should in turn be aligned with project milestones.

- Outline the look and feel that the project wants to achieve: can it be expensive and high quality or does it need to appear cheap and cheerful? This decision will depend on what the project is setting out to do, the brand of the organisation and budget available.

- Who will sign-off the design work and what will the process be? The designer will need to understand the sign-off process and factor it into his or her planning.

- Budget: provide the budget if this is required (if using in-house resource this may not apply).

Vignette: Project Vision

Sir, I'm helping to put a man on the moon.

Vision statements should be just that – a vision of the solution that the project is going to deliver. What will it feel like? What will it look like?

The famous story of President John F. Kennedy's visit to NASA headquarters illustrates the role of vision. On his visit he met a janitor who, when asked by Kennedy about his work simply said: 'Sir, I'm helping to put a man on the moon!' Now whether that is true or not, it makes the point that a vision should be:

- inspiring;

- forward looking;

- simple;

- concise;

- resonate with the project team and stakeholders;

- unambiguous.

Visions matter because they give focus. Organisations use them to inform their corporate strategy. There shouldn't be a place for activity that doesn't contribute to the vision. So it follows that a project will have been established to deliver an aspect of an organisation's vision or facilitate the achievement of the vision.

The project communicator needs to know and understand the vision of the organisation of which the project is a part, as well as any mission statement and corporate values because project communication should be aligned with these. If in any doubt, seek guidance from the central corporate communication team (or marketing communication which may have responsibility for brand values).

In addition to a vision, at the organisational level there may also be:

- A mission statement. These usually explain what the organisation actually does – its more about its present state than its future state.

- Values: these are behaviours and ways of working that are core to the way the organisation operates.

- Brand values: what customers can expect from the organisation and its products.

- Strapline: a concise, easy to remember and recognise statement that sums up things about an organisation and its values. It can also be called a tag line or slogan.

Developing a Project Vision

Responsibility for the creation of the vision probably won't rest with the communication function but it needs to be involved. The vision needs to be communicated and needs to be crafted with this in mind.

The best visions are developed collaboratively. People are more likely to buy in to the vision if they have helped to create it, plus the vision is more likely to be a realistic reflection of what the project can achieve. It can be easy to be too ambitious with vision statements and over-promise what the solution will deliver. Bringing in some stakeholders to help introduces an outside perspective which can be helpful. At this stage of the vision process, the role of the project communicator can be to:

- help ensure that other voices are heard in the process;

- advise on how the vision may be perceived by those who haven't been able to get involved in its formation;

- make sure it is written in Plain English avoiding jargon and acronyms;

- check that it is aligned with any other relevant vision statements (for example at the organisational level).

Good vision statements are specific to the project. A vision that is very general and could apply to any project won't inspire or bring focus. Every project wants to be the best, well respected, deliver on time and to budget, put customers first and so on. Take the following vision statement:

*Our vision is to be earth's most customer centric company; to build a
place where people can come to find and discover anything they might
want to buy online.*

Many people could guess that this belongs to Amazon.

It is concise, written clearly and very specific to the brand. Aim for the same with
the project vision. Keep it short – some project visions go on for several paragraphs
and sometimes pages. This isn't necessarily wrong, but the key thing is that it can be
summed up in a couple of sentences and is easy for people to explain. A vision that
can't be explained without going back and checking the document isn't going to be
effective. Visions like this will end up filed with all the other project documentation
and never looked at again. It can be helpful to share powerful and inspiring visions
such as the Amazon one during the development process to show they can be made
to work.

The vision must be unambiguous. This can be hard to achieve as people will always
interpret something in the light of their own experiences or world view. However,
testing of the vision with project team members and stakeholders can go some way to
overcoming this. Even when a vision has been developed collaboratively, it can still pay
to test it outside the group that developed it.

The development process can take time and be challenging, but this is to be
expected. It is often through this process that differences of opinion or understanding
are drawn out, which is helpful as they can then be addressed. Everyone involved in
the development process should walk away with a shared understanding of what the
project is there to achieve.

Vignette: Communication Theory

There is nothing either good or bad, but thinking makes it so.

Shakespeare's *Hamlet*

Communication must be easy, after all everyone communicates so how hard can it be? Surely it's a 'soft skill'? It's certainly not as difficult as building an IT system or relocating a factory – is it?

Well yes, everyone communicates everyday but an organisational, managed communication process where there is a desired outcome is difficult to get right and anything but a soft skill. This is an interesting area of theory and this Vignette can only give an introduction to some of the more useful concepts. Further reading will be needed to understand them more fully. However, an appreciation of the richness of communication will in itself lead to better communication highlighting as it does the folly of a 'one-size-fits-all' approach and the misconception that communication is easy.

One of the earliest models of communication was drawn up by two telephone engineers – Shannon and Weaver – back in the 1940s (see Fig. 4.3). Their model was linear and based on the way a telephone worked, that is, one simply had to send a message along a channel, and it would be received and then understood at the other end. Of course the communication process is actually much richer than this and all sorts of things influence a message between sender and receiver. Fortunately the theory of communication has moved on since the 1940s but all too much of communication practice is still rooted in this linear model.

It is a mistake to think that because a message has been sent it has a) been received; b) interpreted in the way intended; and c) brought about the desired change in attitude or behaviour. It was George Bernard Shaw who said: 'The greatest problem with communication is the illusion that it has been accomplished.'

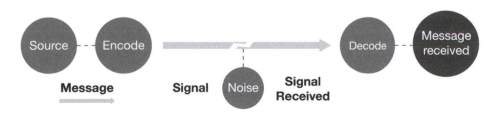

Figure 4.3   **Shannon and Weaver's early model of communication**

Source: Shannon and Weaver (1948), 'A Mathematical Theory of Communication'. *Bell System Technical Journal*.

Most people would agree that communication is rich and complex, yet still much organisational communication follows a linear model and assumes that simply by sending out a message a desired result will be achieved. Project managers may complain that stakeholders don't understand the project and what it is setting out to do. However, there is really no such thing as 'misunderstanding' a message. Someone may understand it differently to the way intended by the person who sent it, but that doesn't make them wrong. Looking at communication from this perspective puts the onus firmly on the sender of the message to understand the perspective of the receiver – to put themselves in his or her shoes. And of course, everyone wears different shoes! However, this is what makes a communication role so challenging and interesting. So, how does communication actually work?

There are a lot more factors in play during the communication process than Shannon and Weaver's model acknowledged. Many things influence the way that a message is interpreted and some of these are captured in Table 4.4.

Table 4.4   What influences the way that a communication is received?

Influences	Relevance for project communicators
The recipient's perception of the sender.	The project leadership team and the project itself need to be trusted. If they aren't, then communication can be met with cynicism.
	Trust can be difficult to maintain on projects when deadlines and scope change. The important thing is to keep the conversation going and ensure that if a commitment is made to do something then it is done and if not, stakeholders are kept informed with a rationale for the change. On a similar note, things shouldn't be done without telling people, this will result in suspicion.
	Trust is even more important as people rely more and more on social media channels for information. They are less likely to listen to traditional authority figures and more likely to look for authentic, trusted sources.
The channel used to send the message and the recipient's perception of it.	The channel is an intrinsic part of the message. Important messages – for example about people's jobs – should be delivered face to face. Sending sensitive or important information by email for example, can make it seem as though the project doesn't really care about the recipient.
	The method of communication should be matched carefully to the content of the message to ensure that it is appropriate.
The world view and opinions of the recipient.	Everyone selects media according to their own world view. People are less open to different perspectives than they like to think. For project communicators this explains why opinions are hard to change simply through one-way communication. For example, somebody may hold the view that all employers are out to exploit employees. That is a hard attitude to change and any communication will be seen through this lens.
The views of others.	People may seek the views of others before they form an opinion. This may be a friend, work colleague, journalist or blogger.

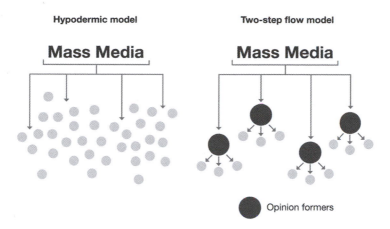

Figure 4.4   Mass communication models
Source: McQuail, D. and Windhal, S. (1993) *Communication Models for the Study of Mass Communication*, London: Longman.

Mass Communication Theory

Mass communication is the term given to communication that targets large audiences – for example printed media such as newspapers and magazines. It is a one-way form of communication. The mass media is very good at telling people what to think *about*, but, because people consume media that reinforces their existing 'world view' it is less good at persuading people *what* to think. Like the linear model of communication, this is a very simplistic view of communication. It suggests that a message can be sent directly to lots of people at the same time and it will be received in the same way, or that it is received and interpreted by others before being passed on to a mass audience (the two-step flow model). This is shown in Fig. 4.4.

Much communication within organisations is based on this mass communication model. Newsletters, intranet stories and traditional conferences are examples. Understanding the limitations of a mass media approach is important, because an over-reliance on this as an approach alone is unlikely to be effective when a change in attitude or behaviour is required.

One-way versus Two-way Communication

The definition of one-way communication is quite straightforward – messages are simply delivered, there is no feedback loop and so the sender has no knowledge of whether the message was received and, if it was, how it was interpreted.

Two-way communication is more complex. Many communication methods are termed two-way simply because a conversation takes place, but this does not necessarily mean that it actually is two-way. True two-way communication involves a willingness on both sides to adapt their position as a result of the dialogue. Tactics such as question and answer documents for example are one-way because they are imparting information.

There is a place for both and it is important to understand the difference so that the right strategy can be chosen for the communication objectives set. Identifying the need for two-way communication but then rolling out a tactic that isn't truly two-way will result in a failure to achieve the desired outcomes.

Personality Approaches to Communication

Understanding personality types can be helpful in designing effective communication. This Vignette points to one of the most interesting from a communication perspective: Myers-Briggs. The Myers-Briggs Type Indicator (MBTI) is a profiling system that measures how people view the world and make decisions. Many organisations use this with staff to help understand team dynamics, but it is also very useful for the communicator. (Further reading will be required if it is to be used effectively.)

An understanding of MBTI and preferred communication types can inform one-to-one communication but also communication targeting groups. Typical differences in communication style can be a preference for detail compared to a preference for theory and concepts

As such it can help the project communicator in a number of ways:

- in personal one-to-one communication with peers, senior colleagues and stakeholders;

- designing communication approaches that will appeal to stakeholders across a range of typologies;

- guiding project spokespeople in how to recognise their own communication style and adapt it as appropriate to the communication situation.

Understanding the communication preferences of another can be a revelation and help to avoid conflict. Take for example the scenario where a project manager who has a preference for detail is working with a communicator who tends to talk in concepts:

> *Project manager: 'Which stakeholders received our latest communication?'*

> *Communication lead: 'Everyone.'*

> *The project manager, exasperated, wonders why her communication lead is being so evasive.*

> *The communication lead, annoyed, wonders why the project manager feels that she needs to check up on him all the time.*

> *The communication lead later finds out about their MBTI profiles. Next time the project manager asks the question he responds by saying: 'Everyone on our stakeholder list received it, that's 200 in total covering managers down to grade B in the finance and procurement communities.'*

> *'Thank you, that's great,' says the project manager.*

> *'You're welcome,' says the communication lead.*

This is a demonstration of the value of MBTI on an interpersonal level, but the same can apply when communicating with groups who may have a preferred communication style. It is also useful in leadership communication. Even the best leader may find that he or she is alienating colleagues because of a tendency to communicate in a particular style. Recognising this and making a conscious effort to adapt to other communication preferences can lead to more engaging leadership communication.

Changing Behaviour

Many projects require changes in behaviour in order to realise their benefits, for example different ways of working. Appreciating the complexity of the communication process brings with it an understanding of why changing behaviour through communication is more difficult than simply sending out a message. Theory proposes that people go through a number of steps (Wilcox et al. 2005). Table 4.5 suggests how communication can aid this process.

1.   Awareness

2.   Interest

3.   Evaluation

4.   Trial

5.   Adoption – idea integrated into belief system, 'I read...becomes I think...'

Table 4.5   How communication can support people to adopt a change

Step towards change	Practical step
Awareness	One-way communication techniques and channels such as a news story, poster, newsletter or intranet. Provide accurate information.
Interest: people seek more information	Provide access to more detail. For example, a follow-up feature story, more in-depth detail online, inclusion in team briefings with more details provided as the basis of discussion. Invite people to get involved in shaping the change.
Evaluation: views sought from others	Create champions who have more information, support the changes and can discuss with colleagues, facilitate others giving their views publicly perhaps through a discussion forum, organise focus groups where opinions can be shared.
Trial: the ideas are tried out with others, saying 'I read...'	
Adoption – idea integrated into belief system, 'I read...becomes I think...'	

5

Selecting the Right Channel and Tactic

How something is said is as important as what is said. The method of communication actually becomes part of the message and so needs to be appropriate for the content. Imagine being made redundant by text message, sending the message in this way shouts disrespect, very different from a one-to-one meeting in a supportive environment which, while the news isn't good, at least demonstrates respect for the employee.

This is quite an extreme example, but it does make the point how important it is to communicate a message in the most appropriate way.

The method of communication is often described as the 'channel'. Staff newsletters, intranet, internet and team briefings are all examples of channels. Communication channels are different to communication tactics. Tactics are individual pieces of activity such as an article in a newsletter, a page or story on the intranet and a message or theme for a team briefing.

Different channels have different characteristics and as well as matching the message the channel must match the strategy that has been set. For example, if the strategy is to simply raise awareness then a one-way channel such as a newsletter may be fine; if the project is introducing significant change and people need a deeper understanding then a workshop may be the answer.

All channels have their advantages and disadvantages and it is a question of weighing these up and deciding which will best.

This chapter discusses different ways to communicate and includes:

- one-way and two-way communication methods;

- the importance of managing channels;

- a channel selector: a detailed discussion of different tactics, their advantages and disadvantages;

- the role of line managers;

- communication on a budget;

- using social media.

The Vignette at the end discusses working with the media.

The Difference between One-way and Two-way Channels

One-way communication channels don't invite feedback – they are largely about pushing out information. This doesn't mean that they aren't of value; there will be many occasions when the task will just be to let people know things. Keeping people informed is important because without accurate and timely information about the project, they won't be able to get involved fully because they won't know enough about what is happening.

Two-way communication channels invite feedback and have a mechanism in place to take that feedback on board. Genuine two-way communication is about much more than just providing answers to a question. For a communication channel to be truly two-way the feedback from stakeholders must be listened to and the potential for it to be acted on exist. Never pretend that the project is seeking feedback if it doesn't intend to do anything about it, this undermines trust and it is better not to seek feedback at all (see Figure 5.1).

CHALLENGE OF TWO-WAY COMMUNICATION

Many channels have the potential to be two-way but a one-way approach is still adopted. For example a team meeting where the manager just tells people things with no opportunity for discussion or feedback is a one-way piece of communication. Again, this is fine, but if this is the only approach that is taken it is a wasted opportunity to have a valuable conversation with employees.

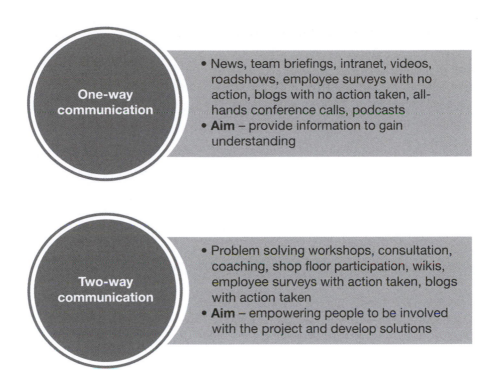

Figure 5.1   **One-way and two-way communication**

It can be difficult to get project managers and sponsors to buy into a genuine two-way dialogue – they often fear that they will be expected to change the strategic direction of the project when it has already been decided. The concern is that an expectation will be created with stakeholders that can't be fulfilled. This can be overcome to an extent by ensuring there is a two-way dialogue right at the start while the strategy is being formulated and ensuring that project leaders are comfortable saying no to ideas.

Another blocker to the two-way approach is that it can seem overwhelmingly difficult to engage with all stakeholders. In an ideal world, this would be something to strive for but the project communicator has to be pragmatic and probably engage with a sample of the stakeholder population instead. This sample needs to be drawn from across the range of stakeholders and an appropriate methodology developed to ensure fair representation. (A 'sample' means a portion of the group of stakeholders.)

Channel Strategy and Management

One of the first principles of good project communication should be that channels are managed effectively. This simply means being clear about what channel is used for which type of content and applying it consistently. This can be included as part of the communication strategy which will help to reinforce the principle.

Having a channel strategy matters because it helps project team colleagues and stakeholders to:

- categorise the communication messages coming from the project;

- manage their time, giving priority to the most important messages;

- think less – they will already know if a message is essential reading or for information simply by the channel through which it is delivered.

Project communicators will need to guard the channel strategy fiercely and not allow it to become diluted or the result will be confused stakeholders. For example, suppose that an 'all project team' email directly from the project manager's personal email is the channel that is used to communicate important strategic information. In this scenario to suddenly send an email from the project manager about the company Christmas party or a team football match would be inappropriate – recipients will no longer know what to expect from that channel. Far better to include this social type of information in a weekly team bulletin or to mention it at a weekly informal face-to-face briefing.

For the same reason it is also important to respect the channel strategy of other communicators, for example on other projects or at the corporate level in an organisation. This can be a cause of conflict when a project asks for its content to be included in a channel owned elsewhere, for example a central corporate intranet, and this request is refused. However, this decision should be respected as it is usually being done to protect the integrity of that communication channel. In these circumstances, the project should work with the channel owner to see if the story could be made more suitable for the channel, or to see if there is a more appropriate channel that could be used.

Line Managers as Communicators

When a project is introducing something new into an organisation, line managers (or supervisors, middle managers and so on) are an important channel. Research has shown time and time again that staff like to discuss important messages with their manager, face to face. However, a common complaint from communicators is that managers don't deliver messages very well – they aren't consistent, they make the message negative or they just don't do it at all.

Managers' reluctance to engage in employee communications may be the result of a number of factors:

- previous or current lack of support (for example through training, messages and communication materials);

- ambiguous and confusing information that they feel uncomfortable delivering;

- lack of personal confidence;

- the view that it isn't their job;

- too many other demands on their time;

- an instruction to simply 'tell' rather than involve by facilitating discussion with the team with the opportunity to shape decision making;

- concern that they will have to 'sell' a message that they feel they can't justify.

To help overcome some of these challenges, project communicators can support effective line manager communication by:

- briefing line managers thoroughly – face to face if possible. Give them the opportunity to ask questions and provide input into the communication messages. If they have been involved they are more likely to want to discuss the messages with their teams;

- leading by example – senior stakeholders and project leaders who are already supportive of the project should lead by example with their own teams;

- emphasising an involvement approach, rather than a 'sell' approach. Managers can feel uncomfortable if they are expected to 'sell' a message that does not seem to have any direct benefit for their team members. Ensure that they understand that their role is as a facilitator rather than a salesperson. Explaining and discussing a message is easier than justifying something with which they may not agree themselves;

- ensuring that processes are in place to capture and respond to feedback. You will quickly lose the trust of managers if the feedback from their team is never responded to;

- provide clear, structured content for managers to base their conversations on, but don't overload them – three or four key messages and some suggested questions to ask is plenty;

- work with the central internal communication team to get your project messages into any existing team briefing process. Remember to make sure you capture the feedback and can respond to it;

- seek the support of senior project sponsors in getting communication to be a priority for managers within the organisation. This can help lead to investment in communication training.

Communication on a Budget

Effective communication does not mean having to spend a lot of money on glossy collateral – in fact less is often more in communication. Thoughtful planning is the first step. Thinking carefully about the audience and what they want to know results in targeted communication interventions rather than a scatter-gun approach which is always going to be more expensive in the long run.

When funds are limited, resources should be prioritised around planning and strategy setting, otherwise money may be wasted on activity that won't deliver the results needed because it hasn't been thought through.

There are a number of ways to deliver good communication when funds are limited:

- Use toolkits and networks. Identify people who can help to deliver the communication strategy. They don't need to be professional communicators but should be keen and interested in communication. Spend some time taking them through the principles of good communication and the project communication strategy. Equip them with a toolkit containing things like key messages, a plan to follow, evaluation forms and any collateral. Keep in touch with them regularly and ensure that they feel supported. They can also be a valuable 'eyes and ears' for the project. As these people will probably be taking on communication on top of their normal workload, explore whether it is possible for them to receive some form of reward and recognition for their work. The other advantage to this approach is that the network can tailor communication messages and activity to the stakeholder groups with which they are working which is good practice even when budgets aren't any issue.

- Join up activity with other projects or central corporate activity. This can save resources and is also an effective, best practice communication approach, helping to tell a joined-up story for people.

- Consult lessons learned from previous projects. If something didn't work before money and time can be saved by not making the same mistake.

- Evaluate throughout the life of the communication activity. If something isn't working then it doesn't make sense to continue with it. Remember too that if something cheap isn't working, then it isn't cheap – it's a waste of resources.

- Make the most of technology – but only if it is right for the audience. There is no point running an online campaign if the project stakeholders have limited access to email or the internet or aren't users of social media.

Social Media for Project Communication

Social media allows for fast communication, collaboration and feedback making it seem ideal for project communication. However, the rules about using social media for communication on projects are the same as for any other form or communication and that means being clear about the objective and understanding the audience first.

Social media is the term used to describe communication technologies that enable people to share content, comment on other people's content and get involved in communities of like-minded people. The content is often 'unmediated' meaning that it isn't usually edited by anyone else before publication, although some technologies such as blogs enable content to be moderated. Examples of social media include Facebook, Linkedin, Twitter, Wikipedia and within organisations, Yammer and SharePoint.

What social media enables is direct conversations with stakeholders. Organisations can bypass the traditional 'gatekeepers' such as newspaper and broadcast journalists and talk directly.

COMMON PITFALLS WHEN USING SOCIAL MEDIA

- Putting the technology first. It is easy to focus on the technology rather than the content and the audience. Social media tools might be just what is needed, but they may equally well not be. The starting point should be the objective for the communication and an understanding of the audience.

- The audience isn't ready for social media. Check that your stakeholders can access social media and are using it. If they aren't using it that doesn't mean that it isn't right for the project, but it may mean that other channels are needed initially until people feel comfortable using it.

- The organisation isn't ready for social media. Social media is all about unmediated, peer-to-peer communication. People can express their views quickly and easily. The organisation needs to be comfortable with this and willing to enter into a dialogue. Old top-down, command and control style communication doesn't lend itself to social media and will undermine its credibility. The culture of the organisation needs to be right if social media is to be used to best effect.

- Starting what can't be finished. Project team members will have to make time to engage with social media – perhaps responding to questions, blogging and so on. It is easy to start out with enthusiasm; the trick is to maintain it. Project communicators can assist here by helping to introduce some structure: a plan of what content is needed and when, scheduling time in people's diaries, suggesting ideas for content and helping with the actual posting. The key is to make it as easy as possible for project leaders to participate. Try to make it enjoyable too. People will be flattered if lots of team members or other stakeholders have read their blog, for example, so make sure that they are seeing the numbers and the feedback. This might sound as though the spontaneity that is often a feature of social media is lost, but this isn't the case – there is still room to respond to events and changes outside of the content plan.

- Content that reads like a highlight report rather than authentic, engaging content. Authenticity is important when writing content for social media. Get project managers and sponsors to write their own content.

SOCIAL MEDIA FOR THE PROJECT TEAM

Technologies that enable collaboration, quick dissemination of information and the building of communities of interest can be great ways to communicate across a project team – particularly if the team is dispersed. Another thing about using social media within project teams is that information can be shared quickly and in an understandable way. Wouldn't it be great to get the project/programme manager or senior sponsor to blog before and after the monthly board meeting? Project board meeting minutes, highlight reports and so on are all essential but don't always make the most exciting read. A quick personal view on key decisions that will be discussed and the outcome could be welcomed by the team.

Of course, this means project leaders being comfortable with sharing personal views and communicating in a more informal way. This is where the project communicator can help. Help doesn't mean writing the content for the project leaders. It means coaching them in the use of the most appropriate writing style, helping them to understand how to strike the balance between being open and honest and not divulging commercial information or other sensitive content.

Other ways to use social media within the project team include:

- Wikis can enable collaboration. Wikipedia is the best known example of this technology. Content uploaded to these platforms can be edited by anyone with the necessary permissions. Users can collaborate on documents or collect background information on a topic.

- Blogs and microblogging are a great way to keep the team informed about decisions and changes.

- Every project needs a 'who's who'. Many platforms allow the building of profiles. Encourage team members to upload pictures and enough information about themselves to help colleagues get to know them.

- Remember too that it is fine to use a mix of traditional channels – posters, team information boards in the coffee area – and social media, it all comes back to understanding the profile of the project stakeholders and having a clear objective in mind from the outset.

Before introducing social media for the project team, it is helpful to understand the profile of the team and how likely they are to embrace it. Playle (2012) suggests thinking about the following:

- Team members' current use of social technologies: this will indicate how ready they are to embrace such technologies.

- Attitudes to privacy: this will influence what activities online will be acceptable or unacceptable.

- Access to technology: project team members without easy access to technology can feel alienated if everything is communicated in this way.

- Attitude towards the organisation/project: do team members feel confident in expressing ideas and opinions in such an open way?

The successful use of social media as a communication tool relies on the project and the organisation of which it is a part being comfortable with open communication and happy to release some control. Where this isn't the case, careful thought needs to be given to whether social media is the right solution. This doesn't mean ruling it out altogether but maybe introducing it slowly, and allowing confidence to grow before moving on to the next step.

Summary

There are advantages and disadvantages to every communication channel. Table 5.1 provides a guide to some of the most popular channels and gives tips for their use. The channel should always be appropriate for the message, because it becomes part of the message. In addition, it should match the strategy that has been set, for example be either a one-way or two-way method of communication.

Table 5.1   Channel selector

Channel	Advantages	Disadvantages	One-way or two-way?	Good for
		Electronic channels		
Email	Quick Inexpensive Immediate	Can get lost if people have lots of email Distribution lists must be kept up to date, nothing annoys people more than being left off a distribution list	One-way	Creating awareness Getting important messages out fast
Tips for use		• Make the subject line of the email short and relevant to the content. Consider using a prefixes – but use them consistently. For example 'For Action' or 'For Information'. Stakeholders need to know if they must attend to something immediately or if it can wait. • Keep emails short, use links to more content elsewhere if needed – it can be off putting to see paragraph after paragraph of text and the message is less likely to be read. • As with all written communication, ensure the key message is in the first paragraph. • Consider setting up an email account for the project communication team so that this becomes recognised as an official communication channel and isn't dependent on an individual being available to manage the emails. • Think carefully about attachments, particularly when communicating outside the project. Can these be hosted elsewhere and linked? • Stakeholders may not have the facility to manage such large emails as people within the project can. • Many people view email on a handheld device – consider whether the content of an attachment is better copied into the email. It this makes the email look very long, use a hold subheading to make clear the distinction between the covering message and the document content.		
e-bulletins	Opportunity to use imagery and photographs Can be appealing in design Easy to reach a large number of people economically	Like email, can get lost in people's inboxes Requires design and layout skills Can be blocked by some secure systems Not everyone likes reading on screen Need to ensure that it is compatible with assistive technologies	One-way	Creating awareness Sharing a number of stories Telling longer stories

Channel	Advantages	Disadvantages	One-way or two-way?	Good for
Tips for use		Check what IT systems stakeholders are using – even within the same organisation systems can be different and things may not display properly. Different versions maybe needed. It can be helpful to use sections to divide up the content, for example one for latest news, another for people news such as new joiners and another for corporate information. Branding must be in line with agreed guidelines. The bulletin can be introduced with a message from the project manager or senior sponsor. This can be a good opportunity to highlight success and thank team members. Some people will want to print it out. E-bulletins by their very nature aren't designed to be printed – if this is a real issue, consider a PDF version that can be printed. Remember though that the layout requirements for reading on screen are different to print. The traditional print layout of columns side by side doesn't always work on screen – it involves too much scrolling. This can make producing two versions expensive and time consuming.		
Intranet	Should be inexpensive and easy to update – either by the project or a central intranet team Good reference source Opportunity to integrate with other social media	Relies on staff looking at the intranet unless content can also be 'pushed' out Can be dependent on quality of the intranet of which it is a part Can quickly become out of date – resources are required to ensure this doesn't happen	Often one-way but can be two-way if linked to social media with feedback that is listened to	News Information and background Conversation when linked to social media Instant feedback
Tips for use		Consider the right way to use an intranet at different project stages. In the early stages when there isn't much news, it may be most appropriate as a method of providing more detailed background information for people who want to know more in which case it needs to be easy for information about the project to be found. Ensure that the date of the last update is always included together with contact details – probably a generic communication email address. Useful content can include frequently asked questions, profiles of the project team and senior sponsors, project timescales. Explore linking to other projects, this helps to give context and increase traffic from people with an interest in the project. As it becomes appropriate to talk more widely about the project, the intranet can be used more as a news channel. For the intranet to be a facilitator of true two-way communication it has to enable a dialogue and the project has to be willing to listen to what is said and take it on board where possible or explaining if it can't, via the same channel.		

Channel	Advantages	Disadvantages	One-way or two-way?	Good for
Text messages	Quick to do and read	Easy to undermine credibility with messages that aren't important and immediate Can be intrusive Relies on staff having company mobiles or being willing to receive messages on a personal device Supporting technology required	One-way	Important updates Short, timely personal messages Marking key milestones and events Crisis communication
Tips for use	• As with all communication, the language of a message sent by text needs to be appropriate to the channel. This doesn't mean using text speak, but content needs to be clear and brief. A message that runs in to a second text message means that either the message is wrong or the channel is wrong. • A text can be a nice way to let everyone on the project know that an important milestone has been reached, but do this too often and it takes away the impact of the message.			
Recorded audio messages (for example via telephone or podcast)	Ensure consistency of message Easy to access Medium life – can be dialled in to over a period of time or downloaded and played at any time	Relies on suitable technology Presenter may need training and rehearsal	One-way	Informing and updating stakeholders and project colleagues, best when there is something of medium to high importance to disseminate
Tips for use	• The message needs to be delivered by someone who has credibility within the project and/or with stakeholders. • Rehearsal is important. The tone of voice needs to be engaging and appropriate for the message – for example, don't crack jokes if the message is about job losses. This sounds obvious but it is easy to get the tone wrong. Ensure that the presenter allows enough time for rehearsal – play back practice recordings until it is felt to be right. • The presenter must remember to introduce him or herself at the start and explain what the message is going to be about. • Sign-off with a summary of the content and advice about where to go for further information. • The content needs to be of sufficient importance to make it worthwhile for people to dial in and listen.			

Channel	Advantages	Disadvantages	One-way or two-way?	Good for
Video-conferencing	Inexpensive once set up Can reach people in many locations Avoids travel costs There can be interaction with stakeholders	Needs effective facilitation Not everyone feels comfortable with the technology	Can be both	Informing and updating stakeholders and project colleagues Debating issues Gathering feedback
Tips for use	• Think about following up a video conference with a facilitated discussed at each location. People may have questions after the video conference and a facilitated conversation about the content with someone on hand to capture the feedback and ensure it is fed back in to the project. This is doesn't need to be a project team member. • Practice with the technology in advance rather than waste time in the session working it out.			
Traditional channels				
Printed newsletter	Can be read at leisure Opportunity to use imagery and photographs Can be appealing in design Can be used to follow up on other channels with more in-depth discussion	Can be difficult to distribute if people are in different locations Will need specialist skills to ensure it looks professional Can be costly Lead times can be long so may not be suitable for important news Can seem a little old fashioned	One-way	Creating awareness Sharing a number of stories Telling longer stories
Tips for use	• The same principles apply to a printed news letter as to an e-bulletin (see above). • There can be more opportunity to use photography and images (because file size and physical space aren't such an issue).			
Company notice boards	High visual impact Can be creative and fun Good for getting short messages across	Professional design expertise is needed Posters can soon become tired Notice boards must be kept up to date, neat and tidy Not appropriate for long, complicated messages	One-way	Raising awareness Short 'call to action' and reminder messages

Channel	Advantages	Disadvantages	One-way or two-way?	Good for
Tips for use	• Ensure that posters are designed within agreed brand guidelines. • Design should look professional. This can be expensive so a solution may be to have a template design that can be adapted quickly and cheaply for a range of messages over time. • Posters can remain on notice boards for some time. This means that messages can become out of date and give a poor impression of a project – particularly if one is produced to announce a date that then slips!			
Frequently asked questions (FAQ) document/ question and answer sessions	Consistency of message Contributes to stakeholders feeling well informed Can provide a quick response to correct rumours	Needs regular updating to maintain accuracy Achieving ownership and sign-off of answers can be a lengthy process with the answer possibly being out of date by the time it is approved Question and answer sessions can be dominated by one or two voices with others being unwilling to speak up	One-way	Addressing concerns and dispelling myths and rumour Enabling a consistent message about key issues to be heard
Tips for use	• FAQs and the answering of questions are often thought to be two-way because there is a conversation. But actually, they are really a way of providing information, so are one-way. • They are very useful, but can be onerous to get signed off within the project with the result that the answer has changed by the time they are published. Social media can help here with project colleagues being encouraged to answer questions about their area. Some help from the communication team may be needed to ensure that they are written in a clear and engaging style.			
Printed flyers and desk drops	A simple flyer can be inexpensive to produce Can have a high impact, for example if placed on desks overnight	Can get moved and lost Distribution can be time consuming Requires design and print	One-way	Desk drops are useful when the message is related to something happening at employees' desks e.g. IT changes Work well as part of a larger campaign to reinforce messages
Tips for use	• Think of the flyer a bit like a mini poster. It has to have impact but can contain more information than a poster. • Ensure that there is a 'call to action' and contact information. • Think about how it will be used – can it be thrown away as soon as read or does it need to be designed to be kept? Flyers generally have a short shelf life, but if something longer is needed then the paper quality needs to be considered and this can raise costs.			

Channel	Advantages	Disadvantages	One-way or two-way?	Good for
Team meetings	Feedback can be gathered and response to feedback shared Personal and interactive	Highly dependent on the skills of line managers in running the meeting	Two-way	Informing Giving people a voice Gathering feedback Promoting understanding
Tips for use	<ul><li>Give managers support and materials to work with. Encourage managers to discuss topics with their teams rather than try to 'sell' the message.</li><li>Ensure that any feedback captured is considered and the outcome fed back to the team. This can be achieved by suggesting two or three key things that a team can discuss. Take care to provide information too so that the team feels well enough informed to offer an opinion.</li><li>Where a project is part of a larger organisation, find out if there is a team briefing process in place and whether it is possible to have project messages included.</li></ul>			
Focus groups	Good for getting shared views and meaning Can generate creative ideas People feel that they have had their say	Need to be facilitated well to achieve benefits, may need to bring in someone to do this that has the right experience There will be a lot of data (in the form of notes or transcripts) to be analysed	Two-way	Creating solutions together Gathering feedback
Tips for use	<ul><li>The most important thing with a focus group is strong facilitation. Without it, some voices will dominate and others won't feel comfortable to share their views.</li><li>Consider using someone independent of the project to do this to avoid any bias within the facilitation. People may also feel happier to express their real views.</li><li>Avoid having too much data (i.e. verbatim transcripts) from the session by capturing key themes as the group discussion progresses. Transcripts can then provide a back up should it be necessary to go back and check what was said.</li><li>Sessions can be recorded, but ensure participants are happy about this first. Explain how the recording will be used. Be aware that this may put people off contributing.</li></ul>			

Channel	Advantages	Disadvantages	One-way or two-way?	Good for
Road shows	Can include demonstrations Opportunity to reach people on shift work, remote sites There can be interaction with stakeholders	Costs involved in staging and travelling for the staff that will run them Time-intensive for those running them Need to be clear by what is meant by a road show. They usually take the form of a static display with people on hand to explain the project and an element of interactivity	Two-way	Informing Raising awareness Demonstrations Gathering feedback
Tips for use	<ul><li>Ensure that there is an opportunity for people to give feedback and ask questions.</li><li>Make sure that the location for the road show is where the target stakeholders are likely to be. This sounds obvious, but setting up a road show in a shopping centre on a week-day afternoon may not reach project stakeholders if they are of working age.</li></ul>			
'Town Halls' (meetings with a large number of attendees)	Opportunity for leaders to meet with a large number of people Increase leadership visibility	Leaders need to have time available because preparation and rehearsal time is essential Venue hire can be costly	Two-way	Informing Raising awareness Gathering feedback Leader visibility
Tips for use	<ul><li>Impose strict limits on the number of slides that can be used in any presentations.</li><li>Make sure that slides can be read from anywhere in the room. There is guidance on effective presentations as part of the Project Communicator's Toolkit at the end of this chapter.</li><li>Introduce interactivity and opportunities for feedback on round tables. This can be much more effective than an open 'Q&A' session where people may be reluctant to voice their views and there isn't time to hear from everyone.</li></ul>			
Floor walks	Opportunity for leaders to meet people on an informal, personal basis Increase leadership visibility	Relies on the leader having good communication skills Can seem contrived with employees feeling uncomfortable	Two-way	Gathering feedback Leadership visibility
Tips for use	<ul><li>Prepare whoever is doing the floor walk well. Think about what issues may come up and be ready to address them.</li><li>Ensure that the leader feels comfortable saying 'I don't know' where necessary and there is a process in place to capture the question and provide an answer after the event.</li></ul>			

Channel	Advantages	Disadvantages	One-way or two-way?	Good for
Weekly 'stand up' (short briefing session for the project team)	Short briefing meetings for the project team are a simple way to keep people updated They have a feeling of immediacy	Needs an appropriate space for them to take place Commitment needed from the project manager to do on a regular basis In an open forum, some people will be reluctant to speak up	One-way, but with the potential to be two way if feedback is taken up	Informing and updating Answering questions
Tips for use	<ul><li>Once the project has committed to the sessions, they must happen as planned otherwise people will put other things in their diary and stop attending</li><li>Schedule them for after a checkpoint or project board meeting so the updates have a sense of immediacy. Agree the content at the checkpoint meeting so the project leadership team are all aware what will be shared.</li><li>Involve other key project team members, not just the project manager. Work stream updates can be included.</li><li>Keep them short. Just ten or 15 minutes should be enough.</li><li>Think about offering a dial in option for staff who are based remotely</li><li>Managers should cascade the update to anyone who couldn't attend.</li></ul>			

Project Communicator's Toolkit: Effective Presentations

Following some simple rules can help presentations to more engaging and effective. The same rules apply here as to other communications, avoid jargon, use Plain English and so on, but there are some additional tips that help to make a difference, particularly when using PowerPoint.

- Never use a font size of less than 18pt.

- Think about the amount of time available for the presentation and the number of slides. Thirty slides for a ten-minute presentation is never going to work, even if each slide only took one minute to discuss it would take half an hour!

- If the presenter has to accompany a slide with the comment 'I know you can't read this but…' then that is a slide that should not be used. If it is essential to share the content that it contains, think about printing it out in a larger size and handing out copies to the audience.

- Use a mix of communication styles – include images for those who prefer visual communication and facts and figures for those who prefer detail.

- Speakers must introduce themselves.

- Rehearse. The degree of rehearsal will depend on the circumstances. If it is a large event with audio equipment being used then a live rehearsal is essential to check equipment and timing. Even a smaller less formal presentation should be run through before being given, even if it is only in a meeting room with a couple of colleagues on hand to give feedback.

- Check the presentation on the machine on which it will be delivered – different versions of software can display things differently.

- At the end of a presentation, sum up the key points and let members of the audience know what the project wants them to do with the knowledge that they now have. If they need to share it with their teams or colleagues, make that clear.

Vignette: Working with the Media

An understanding of the media and how it works is of value on all projects, even those that would seem unlikely to generate any external interest. In fact all projects have the potential to interest the media to a greater or lesser extent, although of course many of them never will.

There are many guides to handling the media and it is a broad topic, so this section is intended only to highlight when it may be necessary to work with the media and explain some of the key principles.

If the project is certain to be of media interest, or indeed plans to proactively seek media coverage to help realise project benefits, then this should be the role of a media relations specialist, either within the project team or the wider organisation. The role of the project communicator is to be alert to potential media interest and ensure that the press office is aware and briefed.

The good project communicator always has the potential for press interest in the back of his or her mind. No story can ever be thought of as only internal.

Media handling can be either reactive or proactive.

- Reactive media relations is when the media picks up a story and comes to the organisation for a response or comment. It is unplanned but can be prepared for.

- Proactive media relations is when an organisation wants the media to carry a story about what it is doing. This is planned activity.

If the project is substantial enough to influence the share price of the organisation then strict rules apply regarding what can be communicated and when. In these circumstances, it is essential that the project communicator works closely with the organisation's central corporate communication team.

Reactive Media Relations

Handling the media can be a pressurised job. Journalists are often working to tight deadlines and demand accurate information quickly; print and broadcast deadlines can't be shifted. For this reason when the press office comes to the project for information it will need to be made a priority. Always give the press office the whole story – this doesn't mean that they will tell the journalist everything, but they need to anticipate what the journalist might ask and be ready to respond accurately.

The press office needs to be alerted in plenty of time if the project might be about to do something that could become news.

It is good practice to provide the press office with 'lines to take' which summarise the key points around the issue and provides suggested responses to any questions that may be asked.

What Makes a News Story?

- Jobs – being created or lost. The media is always interested in stories about jobs, but the level of interest and likelihood of a story being picked up can depend on a number of factors such as whether other jobs been lost in the same area recently and was this high profile? A number of seemingly inconsequential job losses can add up to a trend in the eyes of the media. The political climate is a factor. If the local politician is not part of the present government, the loss of jobs can be used to make a political point. On the other hand, if jobs are being created and the local politicians are part of government, they may want to use the story to promote the success of their policies.

- The environment.

- IT project failures or delays – particularly in government.

- Things that build to make a trend.

- Some form of conflict.

- The significance of the story – how many people are likely to be affected, how much is being spent or saved.

- Human interest, something a bit quirky or different.

Look out for project activities that may inadvertently alert the media and stakeholders to something that has yet to be announced. For example, if an office is to be relocated check that a 'For sale or lease' sign doesn't go up outside or an advert for the premises doesn't appear in the local press or online before people have been told.

Proactive Media Relations

The media can be used to let people know about what the project is doing and how it might affect them. However, there needs to be a strong story and it is important to remember that the way the story appears can't be controlled fully either in terms of content or timing.

Proactive media relations can be used to manage potentially negative stories. If a factory is going to close it is far better to be open about it and announce it to the media in a controlled way rather than hope that they won't find out because they almost certainly will.

As with all good communication, timing is key and the project communication plan should identify the order in which news will be released to different audiences – including the media. In the same way that an important stakeholder will not want to find out project news via the media, the media should hear things direct from the project (or organisation) in a planned, controlled way rather than via a stakeholder (unless the stakeholder has been nominated as a media spokesperson and it has been agreed that he or she will update the media).

6

Creating Plans

Good communication relies on planning.

A good communication strategy is nothing without a plan to deliver it and a plan is of no value without a strategy to guide it. Deciding what communication activity to carry out and when can only be done once the strategic thinking has happened. This thinking takes a little time but is time well spent and avoids a 'scatter-gun' approach.

Planning is also needed to ensure that there are enough resources to run the communication function and to ensure that communication activity will be delivered on time and to budget. The project management office (PMO) will probably need to know what resources will be required for communication and when they will be needed so that this can be built into the project budget.

There are a number of different types of communication plans that may be called for in a project environment and this chapter will look at each:

- The communication tactical plan: sets out what will be done and when to deliver the communication strategy that has been agreed.

- Stakeholder planning (or tracking): which stakeholders will be engaged and when (this may be combined with the communication plan).

- Communication project plan: what needs to be done, by when and with what resource in order to deliver the communication strategy and tactical plan.

- Standalone plans: there will be times when a significant announcement or intense piece of activity needs its own standalone plan.

- Template communication plan for use where communication is being delivered at a local level by someone other than the project communication team.

- Crisis and emergency planning: what to if something goes badly wrong.

- Programme and portfolio-level plans.

This looks like a lot of planning but some plans can be combined according to what works best for the project and some may not be needed at all.

The Case for Simplicity

Plans are there as an aid to delivery – they aren't an end in themselves. The sign of a good plan is when it can be picked up by anyone and provide the information that is needed in order to deliver the outcomes required. For the communication function, rarely, if ever, will plans that run to thousands of lines or pages be needed. Another reason for keeping planning simple is that things will change – often very quickly – and so plans need to be simple enough to be updated to reflect the changes without delay. It is when the planning process becomes more important than delivery that plans fail to be useful. Plans also fail when they are:

- too complex and people don't understand them;

- out of date;

- the design and software used isn't accessible to those who need to see them.

The Communication Tactical Plan

The communication tactical plan sets out what activity will happen and when. The aim with the communication plan is to ensure that there is appropriate activity in place to deliver all the objectives set out in the communication strategy and that all the audience and stakeholder groups have sufficient activity targeted at them. As well as activities and timescales, it should include:

- target audience or stakeholder group;

- objective that is being delivered through the activity;

- key messages to be communicated;

- the person (or team) responsible for the activity.

It can also include how the activity is to be measured. A communication plan does not usually go into the detail of how activity will be delivered, that is, the development of a communication product – this can be included, but it tends to complicate the plan. The communication plan works best when it provides a complete and clear picture of what will be delivered and when. This makes it more useful for project sponsors and stakeholders who will want to know what is going to happen, but probably don't want to know *how* it is going to happen.

Keeping the plan clear and simple makes it easier to identify peaks of activity and possible gaps. For example a quick scan down the 'audience/ stakeholder' column will reveal whether any stakeholder groups are being missed and – if they are – activities can be added.

Consider having a 'plan on a page' version that can be used with sponsors and other stakeholders as appropriate to give an overview of communication activity. This will be welcomed by those with busy schedules and those who want more detail can drill down into the full plan.

THE COMMUNICATION TACTICAL PLAN IN MORE DETAIL

- Communication activity: the plan should explain what communication product or activity is going to be delivered. This doesn't need to be in a lot of detail. It may simply be an article in the staff magazine, publication of a newsletter or a project team briefing. One-off activity as well as ongoing ones (for example, monthly newsletters) should be included.

- Timing: when will the activity happen? This is the date (which can be approximate) when the stakeholder will receive the communication. In the case of a magazine article this will be the date of publication, for a newsletter the date that it is distributed or for an event, the date that it will happen. Timing is a crucial element of the plan for a number of reasons:

- Communication messages may need to be delivered in a certain order. For example, it may be important to talk with senior project sponsors first before something appears on the intranet. The same can apply to managers. If they are expected to discuss something with their team, they should be brought on board earlier so that they can prepare.
- Activity can be co-ordinated. It will be easier to identify opportunities to join up messages for stakeholders which is more effective in both communication and cost terms than issuing several different communications in a short space of time. As well as making the best use of communication resources, this will save time for stakeholders and help to tell a joined-up message about the project.
- Activity can be paced. A steady flow of communication can be better than peaks and troughs. The plan should help to identify where too much is happening all at once or times when there is no activity scheduled.

- Target audience or stakeholder group: an activity may be targeted at one or more stakeholder group and these should all be included in the plan. Ensure that the individuals or groups mentioned here are the same as those identified in the communication strategy.

- Objective to be delivered: every communication activity should be designed to deliver one or more of the objectives set out in the communication strategy. Including these in the plan is a good way of ensuring that there is adequate activity in place to achieve the objectives set and that all objectives are being addressed.

- Key message to be communicated: what message or messages will the communication contain? Again, draw on those already developed and detailed in the communication strategy. Numbering the messages may be useful rather than repeating them verbatim in the plan – it will help keep the plan to a manageable length.

- The person responsible for the activity: it helps to be clear about ownership. Responsibility will usually rest with the communication function, but some stakeholder activity may be the responsibility of others within the project.

There are a number of different ways to display the communication plan. A simple table can work well with activity listed in date order. This makes a good working plan because the focus is on the date which helps with delivery planning. Completed activity can easily be removed or shaded out and new activity added at the end.

Alternatively, use can be made of 'swim lanes' to give a stakeholder view of the plan, with a 'lane' for each stakeholder and activities shown from left to right according to when they will happen. This format makes it easier to check that there is an appropriate level of communication with each stakeholder.

The communication tactical plan does not usually need to be built in project or planning software and in fact there are benefits from it being in a format that is accessible to as many people as possible. Project and planning software may exist only within the project team and the communication plan is a document that others will want to see. For example, sponsors and stakeholders close to the project (perhaps board members) will want to know what activity is planned and their confidence can be gained by sharing the communication plan.

There is a planning template at the end of this chapter as part of the Project Communicator's Toolkit.

Stakeholder Planning (Tracking)

The importance of planning stakeholder activity was discussed in Chapter 3. Some projects may separate the communication and stakeholder roles, but in smaller projects the communication function can take on responsibility for both and even when this isn't the case, they need to be closely aligned. Stakeholder activity must be integrated into wider communication planning. The strategic thinking in relation to stakeholders should sit within the project communication and stakeholder engagement strategy. The additional document that is needed is one that tracks contact with stakeholders, notes issues and captures actions.

Stakeholder tracking documents can be extremely complex containing clever formulas and acronyms in order to analyse and then describe the attitude of stakeholders. If there is the luxury of a reasonably sized, dedicated stakeholder team such documents can be of value. However, they do not need to be so complex and, as with all plans, the important thing is to make sure that it supports the delivery of outcomes.

Essentially, a stakeholder tracker needs to include:

- the name of the stakeholder – this can be an individual or group;

- position/job title if appropriate;

- relationship owner;

- result of any stakeholder analysis (for example, are they high priority);

- stakeholder's area of interest;

- contact made and what was discussed. This can be one-to-one contact but also stakeholder attendance at events, board meetings and so on;

- follow up needed;

- planned future contact.

The purpose of the stakeholder tracker is to ensure that issues raised by stakeholders are addressed and that there is adequate and appropriate contact planned. The tracker can also provide a useful record of messages delivered so when a stakeholder claims not to know something that can be checked against the plan. In the same way, if an important decision is communicated at an event that a key stakeholder did not attend, this can be spotted and an alternative way of delivering the message put in place.

This tracker needs to be living document and will need to be updated on a regular basis with records of meetings held, issues raised and actions taken.

The Communication Project Plan

This is very different to the communication plan itself. This document sets out how the communication strategy and tactical plan will be developed and delivered. It includes timescales and the resources that will be needed.

Using project planning software will usually be required and, because it is unlikely that those outside the project team will want to see this plan, this should not cause any issues. This plan is useful because it identifies the resources needed to deliver the work and also enables the communication plan to be aligned with project milestones. When the plans across the project are combined (usually a function of the PMO) any misalignment will become clear.

Of course, communication may be part of another plan such as business change, but the principles of what needs to be included remain the same.

The project manager/PMO will want to know the key milestones for communication – for example the finalisation of the communication strategy – and these will feed into project reporting so it is important to make sure that the plan is realistic. From a project manager's perspective the important thing will be that the milestones are reached. Of course, the quality of the product is also crucial – there is no point delivering a communication strategy on time if the content is not fit for purpose, so success should not be judged simply through delivery of the communication project plan.

Standalone Plans

Detailed, standalone communication plans are a useful tool to help ensure that important communication milestones are managed well. This type of plan can be needed in a number of circumstances, but is most likely to be needed when:

- there is a major announcement, for example job losses, contract win;

- there is a key decision point approaching and stakeholders need to be engaged.

Major announcements: two principles of communication with stakeholders should be good manners and no surprises. Good manners simply means considering the views and feelings of a stakeholder and designing the communication messages and activity accordingly. No surprises means exactly that – ensuring that stakeholders don't hear important information from an inappropriate source rather than the project. This is particularly important when handling an important announcement (for example, job losses or a contract win). Failing to identify all the stakeholders and informing then in the wrong order reflects badly on the project. It is a common cause of dissatisfaction that stakeholders may have with the project and the communication function.

Decision points: throughout the life of the project there will be times when stakeholders need to be engaged in the run up to key decisions. This may involve members of the project board or stakeholders beyond the programme from whom approval of an important decision is required. It could be the sign-off a business case for continued funding or a decision on design. Whatever it is, the decision is more likely to go in the direction the project needs if stakeholders have been involved in advance.

PLANNING FOR ANNOUNCEMENTS

Developing a communication plan for an announcement is really no different to the development of any other communication plan, it just needs to be a lot more detailed and the delivery tightly controlled.

Step 1

The first step is of course to understand the announcement being made and the gravity of it. Planning will always be needed, but the likely impact of the announcement and number of stakeholders involved will influence the content of the plan.

Step 2

Identify the stakeholders. The priority given to the stakeholders could be different to the priority already set out in the project communication and stakeholder strategy, so a fresh analysis specifically for the announcement is needed.

Step 3

Decide what each stakeholder will want to know. Be prepared to develop messages and products tailored for the different stakeholders.

Step 4

Check for any sensitivities and regulations governing the announcement. A commercial contract win or loss for a public company may be governed by stock market regulations. If the announcement is about jobs, there may be trade union agreements to take into account. In these circumstances, the project communicator will probably need to work with communication professionals at corporate level on media handling and investor relations.

For example, in the UK, announcements that could have an impact on a company's share price must be announced to the stock market first. This means that no other stakeholder communication can take place until this is done. This can make staff communication difficult as employees could hear or see something in the media on their way to work before they have been told. This is unavoidable and needs to be handled by ensuring that as soon as the announcement is public there are communication activities in place to reach employees or that can be seen as soon as they arrive at work. In preparing such communication in advance, ensure that measures are in place to stop the information being leaked.

Step 5

Pick the best channel for the communication. This will depend on the importance of the message, stakeholder and timings. For example, an important stakeholder may need to be briefed face to face in which case it will need to be agreed who does this. It should be the person who owns the relationship wherever possible. It is essential to match the channel to the message, for example, no member of staff would want to hear that their department is to be closed via a message on the intranet.

Step 6

Set the timings for each communication activity. The very nature of an announcement means that it will be made at a particular time. Work back from this, taking into account any deadlines for the channels that may be used. It may be necessary to plan things hour by hour. The important thing is to tell people in the right order – remember that it is about being courteous and ensuring there aren't any surprises. Of course it will never be possible to reach everyone in the order intended – people may be on holiday and so on – but if the project can show that it had everything possible in place for this to happen, the stakeholder will still feel respected.

Check that the communication plan aligns with any other plans, for example activity being schedule by HR(which could be relevant if the announcement is about jobs) or procurement (if the announcement is commercial). All the careful planning done by communication could be undermined in a moment by another part of the business talking to stakeholders in an unplanned way.

Template Communication Plans

Communication is often most effective when delivered locally by those that understand local culture and practice. This can be effective within a large organisation that has a wide geographical reach, different sites or a range of different departments. Those delivering local communication on behalf of the project need not be communication specialists if they can be supported by the central project communication function. The aim of this approach is consistency of message and outcome, but not necessarily consistency of channel. There may be local channels that can be used and these are likely to be more trusted than something that is delivered from a remote project. While consistency of message is important, this does not mean that it has to be delivered in exactly the same language. The whole point of local delivery is that the ways messages are expressed are relevant to the audience. This may be by using local examples and terminology that is meaningful to those stakeholders.

The best way to achieve this is by providing as much support and guidance from the central communication function as possible and a template communication plan is an important part of this. Because decisions about the method of delivery will be decided locally, the plan provided should focus more on the objectives, outcomes and timescales by which things should be completed. It will be up to those delivering the plan locally to 'fill in the gaps' with detail of what activity is planned. Once the plan has been populated at the local level it can be helpful for this to be reviewed centrally. There are a number of reasons and advantages to this:

- The completion of local communication plans should be captured on the communication project plan, so it is important to check that they have been done to the timescales required.

- The quality needs to be checked – do the tactics suggested seem appropriate? Are they likely to deliver the outcomes needed? Have appropriate channels been chosen?

- Timings are aligned, this shouldn't be an issue if timings have been included in the template, but it can make sense to double check to avoid stakeholders hearing things at different times.

- Spotting examples of good practice and innovative ideas that can be shared. There may be some good ideas that could be shared with others and rolled out more widely.

Evaluation and evidence of delivery will be needed to ensure that the implementation of the plan has been to the required standard. This may be something that could be done centrally, or it can be requested of the local delivery team. It is important that the evaluation is done consistently by everyone so that comparisons can be made but this means that there is less room for local input at this stage. If it is to be done locally, then this is best achieved with templates provided centrally, for example a set of survey questions. The evaluation method used will need to allow for each local delivery area to be identified independently so that areas where things aren't going so well can be identified.

Crisis and Emergency Communication Planning

An event that impacts on an organisation's operation, causes problems for the organisation and its stakeholders and has the potential for a negative impact on that organisation's reputation can be thought of as a crisis. Identifying risks and dealing effectively with issues can prevent something developing into a crisis but a crisis can also result from an emergency or major incident being managed poorly. An example of a crisis for a project could be an IT failure that impacts on customers, for example by compromising their personal data or blocking their ability to access important services.

Every crisis or major incident is different, but that doesn't preclude some thinking in advance about how it would be handled from a communication perspective. Far better to be making only tweaks when the crisis or incident happens rather than starting from scratch. Preparation is key.

Crisis management is a specialist area of communication and – if the project carries high risks – it may be sensible to bring in specialist support.

Of course not every project will need a crisis handling plan but a decision should be taken early on in the project lifecycle about whether one will be needed or not. Deciding factors may include:

- Would a failure of any part of the project impact on customers or large numbers of employees?

- Is personal data being handled?

- Is a product being developed that, should something go wrong, harm someone? For example, food, children's toys.

- How much is the project costing?

- Could the project have a negative impact on the environment?

This is by no means an exhaustive list, but gives a guide to the types of activity that may have more potential for crises.

Where the project sits within a larger organisation, a sensible first step is to find out what crisis plans are in place centrally and how the project needs to feed into these. There may not be a requirement to develop a project-specific plan.

Crisis plans will encompass a lot more than just communication, so managing a crisis is very much a team effort both in planning and delivery. For the communication team the focus is likely to be on employees, key stakeholders, sponsors and possibly the media.

The employee crisis communication plan should ensure that employees are kept informed with the same level of speed and accuracy as the media. Employees can be advocates in times of crisis if the situation is managed well. The employee crisis handling contains many similar elements to the media plan and should include:

- An identified spokesperson who will be the consistent voice for employee communications throughout the crisis. This may be someone different to the person handling the press in order to spread the workload.

- The key project contacts for information.

- Out of hours contact details and a deputy for both of the above.

- Who will sign-off any employee briefing messages? As with the press, this has to kept tight and those involved must understand the need for honesty, brevity and speed of response. This can be the same person that signs off media messages.

- How any employee briefing will be handled, for example where will it be held, what equipment will be needed, how will all employees be reached.

- Who will monitor and respond to internal social media? As with external social media, these channels demand a swift, and if possible instant, response.

- Who will update the intranet and how often?

Stakeholder activity needs to be aligned with wider employee communication. It is likely that much handling will need to be on a one-to-one basis with relationship owners taking responsibility for calling stakeholders.

The media crisis handling plan should include:

- who is authorised to speak to the press;

- the key project contacts for information;

- out of hours contact details and a deputy for both of the above;

- who will sign-off any press statements – this has to kept tight and those involved must understand the need for honesty, brevity and speed of response;

- how any press conference will be handled, for example where will it be held, what equipment will be needed;

- who will monitor and respond to social media (for example, Twitter and comments from bloggers). These channels demand a swift and authentic response;

- who will monitor news websites and what the response mechanism will be in the case of inaccuracies;

- who will update the internet and how often;

- who else needs to be involved, for example suppliers, partners, emergency services, local politicians and so on;

- how external and internal communication will be aligned, for example ensuring consistent messaging.

The key point is speed. This doesn't have to mean sacrificing accuracy, but it simply isn't acceptable to spend hours looking for the right person to sign-off a communication message.

Programme and Portfolio-level Plans

Planning at programme and portfolio level should follow the same best practice principles as any other communication plan but will have the added complexity of ensuring that strategies and plans across all projects (in the case of a programme) or all programmes (in the case of a portfolio) are aligned. Both need their own communication strategy and plan.

- From a programme perspective, the planning role is to oversee project communication plans and ensure that they are all aligned and support the programme communication messages and objectives. However, the way that this is achieved will depend on resources. Ideally each constituent project should have its own communication strategy and plan, however if resources are limited, it can work equally well to have one combined plan as long as the activities for each project can be identified easily. Individual project boards will be interested in the communication activity for their project so this is what they need to see and what needs to be reported against.

- At portfolio level, the communication role is to oversee programme communication to ensure that it is co-ordinated and aligned and to provide guidance where appropriate.

Summary

This chapter has taken a look at the various planning documents that the project communicator may need to produce. Careful planning means that stakeholders are engaged appropriately and that consistent messages are delivered to the right people and at the right time. Well planned communication demonstrates that the project is well run and builds confidence in stakeholders. However, while planning is important it should be remembered that the plan is there to serve a purpose and is not an end in itself. As Dwight E. Eisenhower said: 'Plans are nothing, planning is everything.'

Table 6.1   Project Communicator's Toolkit: template communication plan

Date	Activity	Stakeholder	Messages	Objective	Owner	Notes
15 March	Intranet article	All finance staff	To stay competitive we need to modernise our IT systems. The project wants your input into the design. Road shows are taking place to explain more.	By end June, 80% of finance staff to be aware that a new IT system in being introduced. By end August, 60% of finance staff to know what the change means for them.	Communication team working with central, corporate communications.	Corporate communication team has agreed the article.
31 March	Road show	Finance staff in regional office	To stay competitive we need to modernise our IT systems. The project wants your input into the design.	By end August, 60% of finance staff to know what the change means for them.	Communication team.	Demonstration of new IT system to be developed.

7

Research and Evaluation

Communication as a discipline has moved on considerably in recent years to be much more than a 'seat-of-the-pants' soft skill to something that is planned strategically and contributes to business benefits. Without effective research and evaluation, communication is set to fail.

There are three roles for research in communication during the project lifecycle, which are also illustrated in Figure 7.1:

- input research which informs the communication strategy;

- monitoring research during the implementation of communication activity to check if it is working;

- close out research, evaluation of the communication feeding into lessons learned.

Being able to evidence the success of communication activity is what sets good communication practice apart from bad and good communication starts with research.

This chapter makes the case for research and sets out best practice in research techniques. It acts as a guide to selecting the most appropriate research approach for the task in hand and addresses some of the blockers to conducting research in project communication. Research can be highly scientific and many excellent books have been written about it, so this chapter can only provide an introduction to the topic. Nevertheless, there is enough guidance given to enable the project communicator to carry out effective research and evaluation.

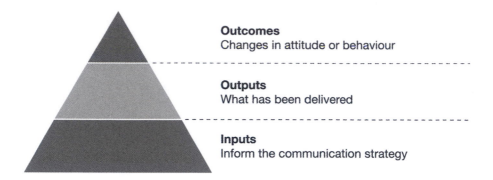

Outcomes
Changes in attitude or behaviour

Outputs
What has been delivered

Inputs
Inform the communication strategy

Figure 7.1   Different stages of research for project communication

Input Research

Research needs to happen right at the start of strategy formation. It is hard to set a sensible measure within an objective if the current position is not known. Of course sometimes the current position will be obvious. If the project is in the initiation phase it is probably safe to assume that awareness is minimal. This doesn't mean however that research isn't needed. It will be helpful to understand stakeholder attitudes before embarking on a communication programme. For example, if the project will be changing ways of working, is there a general acceptance that this needs to happen? Or have stakeholders already been vocal on similar changes? An objective to raise awareness alone isn't appropriate if stakeholders are likely to be hostile, there will need to be objectives around attitude change as well.

Research at the input stage has two roles:

- Understanding the starting position: this will be achieved through a communication audit.

- Setting benchmarks: using research to inform objective setting.

Communication audits are a sensible and fairly essential first step for the project communicator. An audit should seek to understand factors including:

- Which existing channels work best for the stakeholders that have been identified?

- Whether there are any gaps, are there stakeholders for whom no channel exists at present?

- What stakeholders presently think, do or feel.

- The type of communication content that stakeholders are interested in.

- The methods of communication preferred (for example electronic, face to face, print or social media).

The communication audit stage will draw on a number of research methodologies. Original research will probably be required, but existing knowledge – known as 'desk research' – should be exploited first such as lessons learned logs and research done by other projects and programmes. Do this desk research first and then use original ('primary') research to fill any gaps.

Carrying out original research sounds daunting but doesn't need to be and can be as simple as calling up some stakeholders, and asking them for their views, or using the knowledge of colleagues on other projects or in central corporate communication. Where the project is part of a programme, check what knowledge exists at programme level to save duplication of effort.

Research for Monitoring and Evaluation

The communication function needs to be able to demonstrate return on investment. This doesn't have to mean a financial return. On projects, the communication function is there to support the delivery of milestones and the achievement of benefits, so it needs to be able to demonstrate that it has done that. If the function can't evaluate and prove its success why should anyone ever view it as more than a function that simply 'sends out stuff'?

Across the communication industry there is much debate about the best way to evaluate communication activity. In terms of external communication – public and media relations – it has often been based on measures such as 'advertising equivalent' (known as AVE) or opportunities to see (known as 'OTS'). AVE is a tool that measures media coverage, for example a press cutting's physical size is measured and a formula applied to work out how much that piece of coverage would have cost to buy. Opportunities to see draws from advertising and sets out to estimate how many people may have seen a piece of coverage. The issue with both of these evaluation methods is that they say nothing about what was actually achieved. For example, did consumers look more favourably on a product or company as a result of reading an article or seeing a TV interview? Of course being confident that the communication activity alone achieved a result is difficult to judge. Many other influencing factors are in play such as the experiences of friends and family, personal experience or associated advertising. While these debates are ongoing in the world of public relations, there are useful lessons here for the project communicator who should avoid taking the same limited view.

Project communication should not be judged only by how much activity is undertaken, how nice the posters look or how busy the team seems to be. While there is some value in knowing how much activity has been carried out, this is no indicator of quality or outcomes.

Evaluation, like the objectives it is designed to evaluate, should address both outputs and outcomes. An output measure might be how many newsletters were issued or how many visits there have been to a web page. Measuring outcomes involves looking at whether stakeholders thought or did something differently as a result.

Evaluation matters for a number of reasons:

- When done on an ongoing basis, it will identify communication activity that isn't working and enable a change to be made before its too late.

- It feeds into project lessons learned activity, which is more meaningful and useful when based on evidence.

- It proves the worth of communication activity, helping it to achieve the status that it deserves and needs in order to deliver more strategic activity leading to better outcomes.

However, a lack of evaluation is not surprising; there are a number of blockers to effective evaluation of communication and these are discussed in more depth below:

- not knowing what to measure;

- lack of skill in research methods;

- a fear that if something is shown not to be working this will be looked on negatively by the project;

- no interest or support from project leadership;

- no time;

- no budget.

KNOWING WHAT TO MEASURE

The answer to the question 'What to measure' is simple, head back to the objectives that were set in the communication strategy – these are what need to be measured. This emphasises the importance of setting SMART objectives. If the objective has been set properly, it will be clear what needs to be researched. If the objective is for a percentage of a stakeholder community to believe that the project is well managed, then the task is to find out if this is what they think both during and after the communication activity has taken place.

GETTING SKILLED IN RESEARCH

Desk research may reveal that other projects have done something similar or a central corporate communication team may have data that can be drawn on – for example, from an organisation-wide staff survey or stakeholder and media research.

If nothing exists then 'primary research' will need to be conducted which essentially means doing original research specifically for the task in hand.

There are different types of research methodology that can be used (see Table 7.1). Each has its strengths and limitations and it is important to select the approach that is most appropriate to the situation. (Methodology is the term given to the broad approach that will be used for the research, for example qualitative or quantitative. The research method is the actual tool that will be used, for example a survey or a focus group.)

Table 7.1   Different types of research methodology

Type of research	Characteristics	Good for	Associated research methods
Qualitative	Concerned with words and interpretation of what is said. The person doing the research is usually quite involved.	In-depth understanding, analysing feelings and attitudes. Can help to explain why something is happening.	Focus groups, interviews
Quantitative	Concerned with figures and facts. The person doing the research is usually distant from the subject being researched.	Large-scale research, finding out how many people have done something, for example hits on a website. Can help to explain what is happening.	Surveys

Water cooler research

Anecdotal evidence is useful too – there is often no substitute for the intelligence gathered at the water cooler! But while it is useful, treat it with caution because the views expressed may not be representative of the majority. However, this type of informal 'temperature check' can be helpful and provide themes to explore in more detail through more structured research.

Quantitative research: surveys

Surveys are good for:

- capturing a lot of data quickly;

- analysing data quickly and cheaply;

- finding out what is happening.

With surveys, the most important work happens at the start with the design of the questionnaire. Get this wrong and the data will have no value because it doesn't provide the information needed, or people will be confused and unable to complete it. Test the survey on some colleagues first and then on people who know nothing about the project. It is worth spending some time to get it right. Really think about what information is needed and make sure that your questions actually provide the data needed. Some demographic information can be collected, for example, job title, location and age. This can help to identify differences between groups of stakeholders which can be very useful when it comes to designing communication activities. Once the communication activity is underway, it will help to identify any areas where the communication may not be working as well for example within a particular set of stakeholders or geographical location.

Surveys can be done on paper or using online tools. There are lots of free online tools available, although free versions will have limitations. IT compatibility will need to be checked, particularly if working in a secure environment where some outside systems may be blocked.

Tips for good surveys:

- Keep it short – ten questions is probably the maximum.

- Use closed questions as far as possible and provide answers from which people can select. Open questions (where people can write their own answer) take longer to analyse and aren't as well suited to a survey method.

- Write an engaging covering note that includes information on the number of questions and approximate completion time.

- Use Plain English – avoid project jargon and business speak.

- Let people know whether it is confidential and how the data is going to be used.

- Offer to share the results with the people that you asked to respond.

- Set a time limit so people know the date by which they must complete it.

A survey can go to everyone in a stakeholder group but it doesn't necessarily have to, a 'sample' of the population can be selected. However if the population is small, it makes sense to go out to everyone. Best practice on surveys is that a sample size should be a minimum of 30 people (Denscombe 2010). So, if the communication objective is to raise awareness of something – perhaps a new IT system – among finance staff within an organisation, it would make sense to issue a survey to all finance staff. However, if the objective concerned *all* employees, then it may be difficult to get a survey to everyone so the survey could be sent to a sample group of staff. However, not everyone will respond. Response rates to surveys vary and can be as low as 10 per cent. The response rate will influence the validity of the results – clearly the more responses received the better, so if response rates are low, be careful when drawing conclusions from the results – additional checks may be needed.

Qualitative research: interviews

Interviews are good for:

- understanding why something is happening;

- in-depth analysis of a situation;

- exploring in depth something that may have been revealed in a survey;

- revealing themes that can be tested through a survey.

Interviews work well when they are semi-structured. This means having a guide to the questions to be asked, but being prepared to explore other themes if they arise. An interview guide contains some key questions that should be asked in each interview to ensure consistency. However, if a new theme arises in one interview, it can be incorporated in the guide for future interviews.

Tips for good interviews:

- Pick a suitable setting – in the office with the phone ringing and other distractions isn't conducive to a good interview.

- If conducted by phone, ensure that the time has been booked with the interview subject so that they have no distractions.

- Ensure the interviewee knows in advance what the interview is about, how long it will take and how their views will be used. Offer and respect any requests for anonymity.

- Record the interview if possible – taking notes will be difficult and get in the way of asking questions. Get the permission of the interview to do this, some may not be comfortable being recorded and this should be respected.

- Put personal views to one side and try not to lead the interviewee.

- When the questions have been covered, ask the interviewee if there is anything additional that he or she would like to cover.

- Offer to share the final findings.

Qualitative research: focus groups

Focus groups are good for:

- getting a consensus view;

- prompting debate;

- hearing a number of different views.

Focus groups need careful facilitation to ensure that everyone's voice is heard. That can mean managing those who are more confident to speak out and encouraging those who are less inclined to speak up.

Tips for good focus groups:

- Think about having two people to run the session – one to facilitate and the other to take notes.

- Eight to ten people is a good number.

- Use a venue that is conducive to the session and that is away from office distractions.

- Ensure that everyone's voices are heard.

- Plan in advance how you are going to capture the outputs – for example, verbatim comments, or capturing themes on flip charts as you go?

- Put your own views and feelings to one side.

Desk and document research

Using existing research and documents is a cost effective way of doing the initial input research that is needed to inform the communication strategy. There are lots of possible sources:

- lessons learned logs;

- research from other projects or programmes;

- research available from a central communication team such as staff survey results and opinion surveys conducted with stakeholders.

While this form of research is a valid and sensible approach, it does need to be approached with caution and the validity of the research and documents being used needs to be checked. When doing desk research ask:

- Are the findings presented based on a well articulated and justified research strategy?

- If just conclusions are presented, are the actual research findings available to review? Make sure that the findings are based on evidence.

- Did the author of the document have a particular objective in mind when writing it? Was the research presented in a particular way in order to achieve a predetermined outcome? If so, this will have an impact on how useful the research is to others.

- Did the original researcher acknowledge any limitations to the research? If so, consider whether this influences the usefulness of the findings.

The Chartered Institute of Public Relations Measurement Matrix for internal communication

A useful summary measurement principles and practice for internal communication has been developed by The UK Chartered Institute of Public Relations special interest group, CIPR Inside. It provides a useful guide to measuring and evaluating communication. See Figure 7.2.

Why measure? Internal communication is measured to: Establish the value of practice for organisational reputation and success I Generate insights that inform professional practice I Support insightful business decisions I Check progress against plans I Assess overall efficacy.

		How to measure	
What to measure		Questionnaire	Other forms of research
Outputs	**Channels: are they working?** How effective are your newsletters, magazines, intranet, social media channels, e-mail briefings, conferences, "town hall" type meetings, team meetings, project meetings and 1:1s? Is the channel appropriate for the content?	*Access, usefulness, frequency, volume, preferences.*	Content analysis. Ease of reading. Interviews.
	Content: are employees getting the information they want and need? Is communication timely, relevant, accurate and consistent? Is the tone of voice right? Is it open? Is it honest? What are employees interested in?	*How well and how often information is provided. Message recall (for example, using marketing-style analysis). Interest and information levels by topic.*	Content analysis. Interviews.
	Conversations: are people communicating effectively? How well do leaders, senior managers, middle managers, line managers and colleagues communicate, both formally and informally?	*Frequency that people communicate at the level expected.*	Content analysis. Interviews. Network analysis.
	Voice: are there adequate opportunities for people to have a say? How seriously is employee voice treated? Are responses provided to comments and suggestions? Can people get involved in change management and contribute to decisions that support innovation and influence business outcomes?	*Frequency of opportunities, frequency and quality of responses made to expressed voice.*	Interviews. Content analysis (for example, comments in blogs). Focus groups.
Outcomes	**Sentiment: what do employees think and feel about the organisation?** Is communication helping to increase engagement? Are leaders and managers trusted? Do people identify with organisational strategy and values? Are they advocates?	*Understanding and belief in strategy and plans. Perceived organisational support.*	Interviews. Focus groups. Online communities.
	Behaviour: has employee behaviour been influenced by communication? How has it influenced their decisions or behaviour? Are they working more safely, talking more knowledgeably with customers?	*Why did behaviour change, what influenced the employee's decision?*	Pilot or control groups (purposeful or accidental). Network analysis.
	Return on investment (ROI): Have the benefits been identified? Can you isolate other factors affecting financial returns?	*Were the benefits realised?*	Cost (time and resources used), direct return (savings made or profit generated) in a specified time.

Fundamental principles of measurement

- Best practice goes beyond the inclusion of a few communication questions in an annual employee engagement survey.
- Research is part of everyday practice used to establish SMART communication objectives that are output *and* outcome based, linked to organisational objectives that enhance reputation.
- Regular and real-time reporting that includes going beyond basic data is used to find insights from deep analysis.
- Benchmarking helps to put results into context.

Developed by the CIPR Inside Measurement Panel [November 2012]

CIPR
INSIDE

Figure 7.2 The CIPR Inside Communication Measurement Matrix

PRESENTING THE FINDINGS

Everyone wants to be seen as doing a good job, so it is understandable that there can be concern about presenting the results of research that show something isn't working. However, thoughtful presentation of the research findings should help to avoid them being met with criticism. This means addressing head-on any problems that have been found but also discussing how this is going to be addressed. It is always better to present solutions than problems.

Research findings should be presented honestly, after all the whole point of the exercise is to ensure that the communication is successful. Reporting that everything is going well when it isn't (or nobody really knows) will undermine the credibility of the communication function when the project fails to hit its milestones or deliver its benefits because of ineffective communication. It also does a dis-service to future projects that may want to draw on the lessons learned because the same mistakes will be made and the success of those future projects put at risk.

It can be tempting to look for and present only the positives, after all nobody wants what may be perceived as failure to be exposed. However, this will be of no help to the project. The objective of research is to help ensure that communication will be effective and ignoring problems won't achieve this. The key is to present solutions alongside any issues and demonstrate how the intervention has been informed by the research. Of course the communication being off track may be partly or entirely due to circumstances outside of the communication function's control. Picking this up through research and addressing the situation is good practice. Consider whether what has been identified should be included in the issues log. When the communication presents an evidence-based and planned approach it is more likely to be taken seriously and can even set the standard by which other functions will be judged.

When reporting the findings of research and evaluation there are three important factors to include:

- explaining and justifying the methodology chosen;

- explaining and justifying the sample – who was surveyed, interviewed and why?

- the limitations of the research.

These points matter because they are areas where others could criticise the research. While criticisms may be entirely valid, covering these three points addresses any criticism head on and makes it more likely that the work will be respected, as will the author. There is an additional, wider benefit too in that the work will be of more value to others in the future as part of lessons learned.

Those reading the findings of the research may not be familiar with research methodology so it can be helpful to set out the characteristics of the approach chosen and explain why it was considered the most suitable methodology and/or method.

A discussion of limitations simply means acknowledging anything that may have influenced the results. For example, if the number of responses to a survey was quite low, this should be acknowledged so that those reading the findings understand that they need to be treated with some caution. The research method itself will also have limitations. For example with interviews and focus groups there will be always be the possibility that the interviewer or facilitator has had an effect on what has said, even if this wasn't the intention.

Gaining Support for Research and Evaluation

Support for research and evaluation can be gained during the strategic planning stages. It is all part of objective setting. If the project leadership is in agreement with the objectives set, they should be encouraged to hold the communication function to account in delivering against them. This can seem daunting for communicators, but it demonstrates that communication is there to contribute to project success and is a measurable activity rather than a soft skill that nobody really understands and can be seen as dispensable.

Finding Time for Research

Although research takes time and other resources, it will actually save time in the long run. This is because research at the input stage prevents the project embarking on communication activity that is unlikely to deliver the required outcomes. As the communication strategy is implemented, research will help to identify the activities that are less effective or ineffective and these can be stopped and resources diverted into something more effective. So the question should not be whether the project can afford the time and money to carry out research, but whether it can afford not to.

Research on a Budget

Carrying out research and evaluation of communication need not be time consuming or costly, but to skimp on resources for this important area of communication practice is a false economy. What is the point in carrying on with a communication activity that isn't working? That is where the real waste of resources lies. Setting good objectives for communication activity and measuring against them will often result in less communication activity being undertaken, but with the activity that is done being more likely to produce the desired results. That has to make good business sense.

The case for research can be made as part of the communication strategy with budget or resources being allocated to it. There are a number of ways of making research cost effective:

- 'Piggy backing' on research being conducted by other projects or centrally within the wider organisations (where relevant). It may be possible to have questions added to a survey that somebody else is doing for example. For research outside the organisation this could be done through an 'omnibus' survey which collates questions from a number of sources into one survey making it much more cost effective.

- Using free online tools for surveys. As already mentioned, there are a number of free online survey tools available. (Ensure that whatever is chosen is compatible with the systems that stakeholders are using.)

- Surveys are a quick and cheap way to gather data – particularly when using free online survey tools. However, a research method should not be chosen based on cost alone – it has to be right for the research question.

- Could social media be used? The key is to ensure that feedback is gathered in a structured way to make analysis easier.

- Use project team colleagues to gather feedback as part of day-to-day stakeholder engagement.

Summary

This chapter has explained the important role that research plays in the communication planning process and made the case for effective evaluation of project communication. Evaluation needs to look at outputs (how much activity was carried out) and outcomes (what stakeholders did as a result). The results of any evaluation research should always be presented honestly to avoid wasting resources on ineffective activity and to ensure that lessons learned logs for future projects are genuinely useful.

References and Further Reading

Association of Project Managers (2012) *APM Body of Knowledge* 6th Edn, Princes Risborough: APM.

Dainton, M. and Zelley, E. (2005) *Applying Communication Theory for Professional Life*, London: Sage.

D'Aprix, R. (1996) *Communicating for Change, Connecting the Workforce with the Marketplace*, San Francisco: Jossey-Bass.

D'Aprix, R. (2009) *The Credible Company: Communicating with a Skeptical Workforce*, San Francisco: Jossey-Bass.

Denscombe, M. (2010) *The Good Research Guide* 4th Edn, Maidenhead: Open University Press.

Fitzpatrick, L. (2012) Internal Communication. In Theaker, A. (ed.) *The Public Relations Handbook* 4th Edn, Abingdon: Routledge.

Fugere, B., Hardaway, C. and Warshawsky, J. (2005) *Why Business People Speak Like Idiots*, New York: Free Press.

Gregory, A. (2010) *Planning and Managing Public Relations Campaigns* 3rd Edn, London: Kogan Page.

Grunig, J.E. (1992) Symmetrical Systems of Internal Communication. In Grunig, J.E. (ed.) *Excellence in Public Relations and Communication Management*, New Jersey: Lawrence Erlbaum Associates.

Johnson, G., Scholes, K. and Whittington, R. (2008) *Exploring Corporate Strategy* 8th Edn, London: PrenticeHall.

Kotter, J.P. (1996) *Leading Change*, Boston: Harvard Business School Press.

Li, C. (2010). *Open Leadership: How Social Technology Can Transform the Way You Lead*, San Francisco: Jossey-Bass.

Li, C. and Bernoff, J. (2011) *Groundswell, Winning in a World Transformed by Social Technologies*, Boston: Forrester Research, Inc.

MacLeod, D. and Clarke, N. (2009) *Engaging for Success: Enhancing Performance Through Employee Engagement, A Report to Government*, Department for Business, Innovation and Skills, www.bis.gov.uk.

McQuail, D. and Windhal, S. (1993) *Communication Models for the Study of Mass Communication*, London: Longman.

Morgan, G. (1997) *Images of Organization*, Thousand Oaks: Sage.

Myers, I.B. and Myers, P.B. (1995) *Gifts Differing: Understanding Personality Type*, Palo Alto C.A.: Davies-Black Publishing.

Perloff, R.M. (2008) *The Dynamics of Persuasion, Communication and Attitudes in the 21st Century* 3rd Edn, New York: Lawrence Erlbaum Associates.

Peters, T.J. and Waterman, R.H. (1982) *In Search of Excellence*, New York: Harper and Row.

Playle, T. (2012) *Exploring Internal Communication* 2nd Edn, Harlow: Pearson.

Quirke, B. (2008) *Making the Connections: Using Internal Communications to Turn Strategy into Action*, Aldershot: Gower Publishing Ltd.

Ruck, K. (ed.) (2012) *Exploring Internal Communication* 2nd Edn, Harlow: Pearson.

Ruck, K. (2012) *Exploring Public Relations*, Harlow: Pearson Education Limited.

Schein, E.H. (2004) *Organizational Culture and Leadership* 3rd Edn, San Francisco: Jossey-Bass.

Smith, R. (2005) *Strategic Planning for Public Relations* 2nd Edn, Mahwah: Lawrence Erlbaum.

Smythe, J. (2007) *The CEO: Chief Engagement Officer, Turning Hierarchy Upside Down to Drive Performance*, Aldershot: Gower Publishing Ltd.

Tapscott, D. (2009) *Grown Up Digital: How the Net Generation is Changing Your World*, New York: McGraw-Hill.

Tourish, D. and Hargie, O. (2004) *Key Issues in Organisational Communication*, Abingdon: Routledge.

Truss, C., Soane, E., Edwards, C., Wisdom, K., Croll, A. and Burnett, J. (2006) *Working Life: Employee Attitudes and Engagement 2006*, London: Chartered Institute of Personnel and Development.

Waddington, S. (2012) *Share This, The Social Media Handbook for PR Professionals*, Chichester: John Wiley and Sons.

Watson, T. and Noble, P. (2007) *Evaluating Public Relations: A Best Practice Guide to Public Relations* 2nd Edn, London: Kogan Page.

Wilcox, D.L., Cameron, G.T., Ault, P.H. and Agee, W.K. (2005) *Public Relations Strategies and Tactics* 7th Edn, Upper Saddle River, NJ: Pearson Education Inc.

Yeomans, L. (2009) Internal Communication. In Tench, R. and Yeomans, L. (eds) *Exploring Public Relations*, Harlow: Pearson Education.

Index